D0929582

ANNALS OF THE NEW YORK ACADEMY OF SCIENCES

Volume 701

EDITORIAL STAFF

Executive Editor
BILL M. BOLAND

Associate Editor
DENIS M. CULLINAN

The New York Academy of Sciences
2 East 63rd Street
New York, New York 10021

ANNALS OF THE NEW YORK ACADEMY OF SCIENCES

Volume 701

PROMOTING ACTIVE LEARNING IN THE LIFE SCIENCE CLASSROOM

Edited by Harold I. Modell and Joel A. Michael

The New York Academy of Sciences
New York, New York
1993

Library of Congress Cataloging-in-Publication Data

Promoting active learning in the life science classroom / edited by
Harold I. Modell and Joel A. Michael.
   p. cm.—(Annuals of the New York Academy of Sciences, ISSN
0077-8923 ; v. 701)
   Result of a workshop held by the New York Academy of Sciences on
Feb. 12-14, 1993, in Lexington, Ky.
   Includes bibliography references and index.
  ISBN 0-89766-829-4 (cloth. -- ISBN 0-89766-830-8 (paper)
  1. Biology--Study and teaching (Higher)--Congresses.
   2. Physiology--Study and teaching (Higher)--Congresses. 3. Life
sciences--Study and teaching (Higher)--Congresses. 4. Active
learning--Congresses. I. Modell, Harold I. II. Michael, Joel A.
III. Series
Q11.N5 vol. 701
[QP315]
500 s--dc20
[574'.0711]

93-3002
CIP

&/UBP
Printed in the United States of America
ISBN 0-89766-829-4 (cloth)
ISBN 0-89766-830-8 (paper)
ISSN 0077-8923

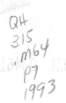

ANNALS OF THE NEW YORK ACADEMY OF SCIENCES

Volume 701
December 31, 1993

PROMOTING ACTIVE LEARNING IN THE LIFE SCIENCE CLASSROOM[a]

Editors
HAROLD I. MODELL AND JOEL A. MICHAEL

Conference Organizers
HAROLD I. MODELL, JOEL A. MICHAEL, ROBERT G. CARROLL, AND DANIEL RICHARDSON

CONTENTS

[a]This volume is the result of a workshop entitled Promoting Active Learning in the Life Science Classroom, held by the New York Academy of Sciences on February 12–14, 1993 in Lexington, Kentucky.

Financial support was received from:

Supporter
GE Foundation

Contributors
Glaxo Inc. Research Institute
ICI Pharmaceuticals Group
SmithKline Beecham Pharmaceuticals

Preface

Perhaps one of the most exciting challenges facing life science educators today is re-establishing the classroom as an active learning environment. This workshop arose from a perceived need to help faculty recognize the advantages of an active learning environment and to provide a forum in which they could begin to explore the issues related to promoting active learning in the classroom.

We hope that this volume will serve as an intitial resource for faculty interested in exploring the excitement of an active environment for learning, and that it will encourage future workshops focused on life science education.

We thank the participants for their enthusiastic response to the issues raised, the Program Committee of the New York Academy of Sciences, especially Dr. Fleur Strand, for encouraging this effort, and the staff of the Academy, especially Geraldine Busacco and Renée Wilkerson, for helping to make the workshop a success. Finally, we thank all those in the Editorial Department of the Academy for seeing this book through the press.

—HAROLD I. MODELL
—JOEL A. MICHAEL
—ROBERT G. CARROLL
—DANIEL RICHARDSON

Promoting Active Learning in the Life Science Classroom: Defining the Issues

HAROLD I. MODELL[a,b] AND JOEL A. MICHAEL[c]

[a]National Resource for Computers in Life Science Education
Seattle, Washington 98115

[c]Department of Physiology
Rush Medical College
Chicago, Illinois 60612

Anyone exposed to the news media in this country must be aware of the crisis in American education. For more than a decade, the headlines have informed us that something is wrong with the way we educate our children and that, as a consequence, we have become "a nation at risk."[1] Every critique of the American educational scene, from kindergarten to professional school, has agreed that our students memorize too many facts but cannot use those facts to solve problems. Numerous comparisons of academic achievement in a wide variety of disciplines across a wide range of countries has shown that the achievement of American students is near the bottom of the list. As educators we seem to be failing our students, and calls for reform are widespread.

This crisis is as evident in the life science classroom as it is in every other classroom. Whether we examine "biology education in the nation's [elementary and high] schools"[2] or the teaching of pre-clinical biomedical sciences in our medical schools,[3] we find the same kinds of criticisms and the same calls for reform. We ask our students to assimilate information, but we don't require them to use that information. We provide them with too many passive learning experiences (lectures), too many "cookbook" laboratory experiences, and too few opportunities for active learning that can lead to the development of problem solving skills and an appreciation for science as a person. We must change how we teach!

The growing awareness of the need for significant change in American education has occurred at a time when the cognitive sciences and educational psychology are making substantial progress in understanding what learning means and the processes that promote it.[4] While there is, as yet, no specific prescription for assisting life science students in achieving meaningful learning, what has been learned can make a real difference in how and what we teach.

Another important development is a growing recognition that teaching must regain its importance on our college campuses.[5] Teaching is a scholarly activity that can and should be evaluated and rewarded as such. But like all scholarly activities, the results of our efforts need to be communicated to our peers so that our ideas can be critiqued and so that others can benefit from them.

The sponsorship by the New York Academy of Sciences of this "Promoting

[b]Address for correspondence: National Resource for Computers in Life Science Education, P.O. Box 51187, Seattle, Washington 98115.

1

Active Learning in the Life Science Classroom" workshop is, in many ways, the result of recognizing that an educational crisis indeed exists and that there are solutions to be shared by the members of the life science education community. The intent of the workshop was to help participants reevaluate their role as teachers and to make them aware of the most current ideas about techniques to help students engage in the type of meaningful learning experience that we all seek for the life science classroom. It was our hope that the workshop participants, by sharing their own personal experience, would stimulate one another to begin experimenting with new techniques and approaches. Finally, by presenting this issue of the *Annals* to the life science community at large, we hope to help our colleagues become involved in the movement to improve life science education.

In this essay we will frame some of the issues that arise when one attempts to produce an active learning environment. Each issue was the focus for one workshop session and is developed in greater depth in one of the papers in this issue of the *Annals*.

WHAT IS AN ACTIVE LEARNING ENVIRONMENT?

We define an active learning environment as one in which students individually are encouraged to engage in the process of building their own mental models from the information they are acquiring. In addition, as part of the active learning process, the student should constantly test the validity of the model being constructed. The traditional lecture environment, in which an instructor merely disseminates information to a group of students, is not an active learning environment, even when the lecturer attempts to format or structure the material in a way that ought to assist model building. If the lecturer does not require each student to personally engage with the material being presented, active learning is not likely to occur. The traditional laboratory exercise, presumably designed to actively engage students, may also not meet our definition of an active learning environment. If students merely follow the prescription provided by the laboratory protocol, and if no effort is made (either by the protocol or by the instructor who is present during the exercise) to encourage active model building and testing by each student, then active learning will not occur. The fact that the students have been "busy" doing the experiment does not mean that they have been actively learning. To promote active learning, the protocol and/or the instructor should direct the student to focus on the rationale behind each step, asking the student to predict the outcome of the step and consider the implications of the data as they are obtained.[6]

The key to providing an active learning environment lies in how the "teacher" views his or her role in the learning environment. In the passive learning environment of the lecture hall, the lecturer (teacher) disseminates information. However, the physical presence of students as an audience is not essential to the learning that may result; a videotape of the lecture may provide the student with the same experience that is available in the classroom. In contrast, students must be present in an active learning environment. In this environment, the role of the

teacher is to help the learner to learn. This may involve the teacher's dis-
seminating information, but it requires that the teacher assist the individual
student in building his or her own understanding of the material. Thus, the focus
moves from the lecturer (teacher) imparting knowledge, to the student (learner)
integrating the knowledge into an existing personal framework, and the teacher
must interact repeatedly with the student to determine how to help the student
with this integration process. This interaction must not only include the types
of questions usually posed in a rhetorical manner by a lecturer, but also other
response-seeking questions designed to give the teacher some insight into how
the student interprets the information presented. Furthermore, the teacher must
be prepared to alter his or her instructional plan based on the responses received.

Active learning is a process that can be encouraged in all educational
settings, and how this might be accomplished in large and small group settings
will be considered in this volume.

HOW PREPARED ARE OUR STUDENTS?

All instructors make assumptions about the background and capabilities of
their students. In many cases, prerequisite courses are stipulated as entry requirements to our life science courses. It is assumed that if students have
satisfactorily completed the prerequisite courses, they have achieved a mastery
of a certain body of material (facts and concepts) and have reached a certain
level of performance skills (observation, analysis, inference, etc.). However,
these assumptions are seldom verified before a course is actually taught (regardless of whether the instructor's course aims at active learning or not), and
courses are designed as if all of these assumptions are valid.

All too often, unfortunately, student performance on test questions that most
heavily depend on those assumptions' being correct is poor, and we discover
that the assumptions were not valid. In a passive learning environment, it is
difficult for us to discover the errors in our assumptions of prerequisite knowledge and skills. On the other hand, in an active learning environment, these
assumptions are tested on a continuing basis, for if the goal is to help the learner
to learn, we must discover where the learner needs help. If help is needed in
practicing critical skills, then we must provide students with the opportunity to
practice those skills before moving on to areas in which those skills play an
essential role in building understanding.

It is not a trivial task to determine what prerequisite knowledge and process
skills are necessary for any particular course. One task for each of us, then, is
to analyze our courses systematically to determine the prerequisites as we
prepare for our teaching assignments.

It is clear that, in today's educational environment, students are generally not
fully prepared to become life science problem solvers. It may, therefore, be of
considerable utility for the life science community to begin developing more
comprehensive guidelines that define what should be mastered by students at
different educational levels to prepare them to advance to the next level. With
students better prepared at each preceding level, we will be in a position to build

on previously established foundations, thus moving our students to successively higher levels of mastery.

WHAT ARE MY EDUCATIONAL OBJECTIVES
IN THE CLASSROOM?

In the 1970s, many of us were introduced to the idea of setting learning objectives for our courses. These were statements intended to serve as a study guide for students. While faculty may have used the learning objectives they defined as a guide to the content covered in the course, they did not use teaching objectives to guide the manner in which the content would be delivered in the classroom. In a passive learning environment, this omission may have minimal impact on instructor-student interaction. The instructor presents the content in a particular fashion, and it is up to the student to integrate the information into a conceptual framework and learn how to use that framework to solve problems. In an active learning environment, the instructor interacts with the student in a joint effort to help the student integrate the information into a model and then test that model (i.e., solve problems). In this environment, teaching objectives play an integral role in determining classroom activities. If, for example, one expects students to be able to predict what will happen when a physiological system is perturbed (a process-oriented objective), activities designed to provide practice in making such predictions must be included, and these activities must include a diagnostic component to help students determine where in the process they are having difficulty.

Teaching objectives may, in some cases, be similar to behavioral learning objectives. In other cases, however, they may be broader in scope and not necessarily made known to the student. For example, an educational objective may be to help students recognize that concepts applied to one physiological system are also common to other physiological systems (e.g., the determinants of blood flow through vessels and the determinants of gas flow through airways). Regardless of their form, specific teaching objectives provide direction for the form and format of classroom activities.

HOW CAN WE PROMOTE AN ACTIVE LEARNING
ENVIRONMENT IN DIFFERENT EDUCATIONAL SETTINGS?

Active learning requires that students be involved in activities that help them to integrate information into a functional conceptual framework. Many different activities fulfill this requirement, and many of these activities can be used in a variety of educational settings. Having one or more students performing experiments that involve a live preparation is best suited to one educational setting, in this case, the student laboratory. However, an activity in which three students work together to determine the clinical manifestation of a pathophysiological process can be accomplished in an independent study, a small group discussion, or a lecture hall setting. Although the students participate in a cooperative learning environment in each setting, each setting has its own constraints that can result in a different educational experience for the students involved. To help keep these constraints in mind when discussing "classroom" activities, we define two classes of learning environments based on the goal of the instructor-student interaction. A "small group" setting is one in which the intent of the instructor is to meet the needs of each individual student. The instructor interacts with each student to diagnose areas of learning difficulty and provide feedback to help the learner overcome the difficulty. We have chosen the term "small group" because this goal requires the type of one-to-one interaction that can best be achieved in laboratory or small group discussion formats.

We define a "large group" setting as one in which some constraint prevents the instructor from interacting on a one-to-one basis with each individual student. While the instructor may interact with individual students in this setting, the intent is to sample class members or stimulate the group to engage in an active learning process. The interaction may be as simple as posing a question and soliciting an answer from the class by a show of hands, or as sophisticated as having the class work together to explore physiological mechanisms with the aid of a computer simulation.

Although the term "large group" usually connotes a significant class size (e.g., more than 30 students), the size of the class is not the most important defining characteristic. The factor that distinguishes "large group" from "small group" is the nature and intention of the instructor's interaction with the group.

The key to promoting an active learning environment is to keep the student as the focus of the learning process. Activities must be process-oriented and designed to force the student to think about the system under consideration. Whenever possible, students should be required to make a commitment based on their mental model of the system. In this way, the students engage in an ongoing process of testing and refining their mental models.

WHAT IS THE ROLE OF CLASSROOM ASSESSMENT IN AN ACTIVE LEARNING ENVIRONMENT?

To many instructors, the term "classroom assessment" means the midterm and final examinations. After all, these exams are generally taken in the classroom, and their purpose is to assess the students' "knowledge level" at various times during the course. These examinations are certainly important in evaluating individual student progress.

In an active learning environment, however, we are faced with another assessment need. In this environment, the role of the faculty is to help the learner to learn. Thus, we must assess (1) how well the learners are learning and (2) how well we are helping in that process. The assessment process must be ongoing and provide feedback to the instructor to help tailor classroom activities to the needs of the students.

This assessment may take many forms. Responses to content-specific questions may be solicited; in the case of large group sessions, one may solicit responses to more general inquiries related to course concepts or mode of presentation (e.g., What was the most important point made in class today? What did you find most confusing in today's class?); or, in the case of small group sessions, specific feedback related to the form and format of the session may be solicited. In all cases, students must understand that responses to these queries are being solicited anonymously and are not being sought for grading purposes. Furthermore, if the assessment identifies deficiencies, they must be addressed. Thus, ongoing classroom assessment is an integral part of an active learning environment.

WHAT ARE APPROPRIATE LEARNING RESOURCES FOR AN ACTIVE LEARNING ENVIRONMENT?

The goal of promoting an active learning environment is to help students develop their thinking and problem solving skills with respect to the course content. To be consistent with this goal and to maximize the active learning that occurs, the learning resources (laboratory write-ups, problem or question sets, computer-based education programs) produced for the students should encourage students to think about the implications of the facts they are acquiring and to reason from specific facts to general concepts (i.e., the resources should be process-oriented) rather than merely presenting factual information in a didactic fashion.

The contrast in approach can be illustrated by considering two exercises based on the classic student laboratory in which the response of red blood cells (RBCs) to solutions having differing tonicities is observed.

In the first exercise, the student is told that when RBCs are placed in 0.9% NaCl (an isotonic solution), their volume will not change; that when RBCs are placed in a hypotonic solution (e.g., 0.3% NaCl) they will swell and, depending on the tonicity, may burst; and that when RBCs are placed in a hypertonic solution, they will shrink. The student is then asked whether a 1.5% NaCl solution is hypotonic, isotonic or hypertonic with respect to a red blood cell. In this exercise, information is presented in a didactic fashion after which the student is asked to recall the information that was presented.

In the second exercise, the student is told that he can run an experiment, the purpose of which is to learn how cells behave in different osmotic environments. He can choose to observe an RBC after it is immersed in a sample of the selected test solution. The student selects a test solution (e.g., 0.3% NaCl) from the list and runs the experiment (in the laboratory or with a simulation of the system). He is then asked first what happened to the cell and then how the osmotic activity of the test solution compares to that inside the red cell. Upon answering these questions, he is told the appropriate term (i.e., hypotonic, isotonic, hypertonic) that describes the test solution. This exercise is process-oriented. The student runs an experiment of his choosing and makes observations. He must then think about the system he is studying and reach a conclusion about what is responsible for the reaction that he saw.

In the first exercise, the student was actively doing something (he had to indicate in some way that he was ready for the next step, and he had to answer the question), but he was not involved in an active learning exercise. The second exercise, however, did involve the student in an active learning experience. It was necessary for him to test his understanding (i.e., his mental model) of osmotic relationships as he progressed through the exercise.

CONCLUSION

We are advocating the replacement of the passive learning environment currently found in most life science classrooms with active learning environments. This is one approach to addressing the challenge to science education that was voiced by Volpe nearly ten years ago and that has yet to be met:

Public understanding of science is appalling. The major contributor to society's stunning ignorance of science has been our educational system. The inability of students to appreciate the scope, meaning, and limitations of science reflects our conventional lecture-oriented curriculum with its emphasis on passive learning. The student's traditional role is that of a passive note-taker and regurgitator of factual information. What is urgently needed is an educational program in which the students become interested in actively knowing, rather than passively believing.[7]

The promise of the active learning environment stems from recognizing that (1) students must have practice using science as a thinking process and (2) the role of the faculty is to help students learn how to engage in that process.

REFERENCES

1. NATIONAL COMMISSION ON EXCELLENCE IN EDUCATION. 1983. A Nation at Risk: The Imperative for Reform. Government Printing Office. Washington, DC.
2. NATIONAL RESEARCH COUNCIL (U.S.) COMMITTEE ON HIGH-SCHOOL BIOLOGY EDUCATION. 1990. Fulfilling the Promise: Biology Education in the Nation's Schools. National Academy Press. Washington, DC.
3. ASSOCIATION OF AMERICAN MEDICAL COLLEGES. 1984. Physicians for the twenty-first century, the GPEP report. Association of American Medical Colleges. Washington, DC.
4. MICHAEL, J.A. 1989. An agenda for research on teaching of physiology. Am. J. Physiol. 256 (Advances in Physiology Education, 1), S14–S17.
5. BOYER, E. L. 1990. Scholarship Reconsidered: Priorities of the Professoriate. Carnegie Foundation for the Advancement of Teaching. Princeton, NJ.
6. MODELL, H. I. 1991. Designing protocols for student laboratories. Computers in Life Science Education 8: 91–94.
7. VOLPE, E. P. 1984. The shame of science education. Am. Zoologist 24: 433–441.

How We Teach and How Students Learn[a]

LILLIAN C. McDERMOTT

Department of Physics, FM-15
University of Washington
Seattle, Washington 98195

INTRODUCTION

For more than 15 years, the Physics Education Group at the University of Washington has been investigating student understanding of physics and using our findings as a guide for developing curriculum.[1] Recently, our work has focused on the introductory calculus-based course that is required for science and engineering students.[2] Results from our studies, as well as those by other investigators, indicate that the difference between what is taught and what is learned in a typical class is often greater than most instructors realize.[3] This discrepancy suggests the following question: Is there a corresponding mismatch between *how* we teach and *how* students learn? In this paper, we consider this question in the context of physics. However, colleagues from other disciplines should have no difficulty in making appropriate analogies.

TRADITIONAL APPROACH TO INSTRUCTION

Instruction in introductory physics has traditionally been based on the instructor's view of the subject and the instructor's perception of the student. Most teachers of physics are eager to transmit both their knowledge and enthusiasm. They hope that their students will acquire not only specific information and skills but also come to appreciate the beauty and power that the physicist finds in physics. Having obtained a particular insight after hours, days, months or years of intellectual effort, they want to share this knowledge. To save students from going through the same struggles, instructors often teach from the top down, from the general to the particular. Generalizations are often fully formulated when they are introduced. Students are not actively engaged in the process of abstraction and generalization. Very little inductive thinking is involved; the reasoning is almost entirely deductive. By presenting general principles and showing how to apply them in a few instances, instructors hope to teach students how to do the same in new situations.

In recalling how they were inspired by their own experience with introductory physics, many instructors tend to think of students as younger versions of themselves. In actual fact, such a description fits only a very small

[a]This work was supported in part by the National Science Foundation under a series of grants, of which the most recent is MDR 8950322.

minority.[4] Typically, in the United States today, no more than one in every 30 university students taking introductory physics will major in the subject. The trouble with the traditional approach is that it ignores the possibility that the perception of students may be very different from that of the instructor. Perhaps most students are not ready or able to learn physics in this way. Moreover, since most people teach as they have been taught, the standard introductory course may be particularly unsuitable for students who plan to teach at the precollege level.[5]

SOME GENERALIZATIONS ABOUT LEARNING AND TEACHING

The generalizations that appear below are based on results from our research on the learning and teaching of physics.[6] However, the same arguments could be based on findings by other investigators. Similar conclusions have also been reached by experienced instructors who have probed student understanding in less formal ways in the classroom.[7]

1. *Facility in solving standard quantitative problems is not an adequate criterion for functional understanding: Questions that require qualitative reasoning and verbal explanation are essential.*

The criterion most often used in physics instruction as a measure of mastery of the subject is performance on standard quantitative problems. As course grades attest, many students who complete a typical introductory course can solve such problems satisfactorily. However, they are often dependent on memorized formulas and do not develop a functional understanding of physics, i.e., the ability to do the reasoning needed to apply appropriate concepts and physical principles in situations not previously encountered. Our investigation of student understanding of simple electric circuits provides many examples.[8]

One task that has proved particularly effective for eliciting common conceptual and reasoning difficulties is based on the three circuits in FIGURE 1. All have identical bulbs and ideal batteries. Students are asked to rank the five bulbs according to relative brightness and to explain their reasoning.

A correct comparison requires no calculations. A simple qualitative model, in which bulb brightness is related to current or potential difference, can be used

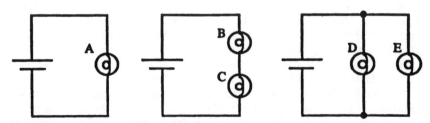

FIGURE 1. Students are asked to rank by brightness the five identical bulbs and to explain their reasoning. They are told to assume that the batteries are ideal. The correct response is A = D = E > B = C.

to determine that bulb A, bulb D and bulb E will be equally bright and brighter than the other two bulbs, which will be equal in brightness to each other (A = D = E > B = C). This task has been administered to more than 500 university students. Almost every possible bulb order has appeared. Whether before or after instruction, only about 15% of the students in a typical calculus-based physics course give the correct ranking. We have obtained the same results from high school physics teachers and from university faculty who teach other sciences and mathematics. Many people who are unable to rank the bulbs properly can use Ohm's law and Kirchhoff's rules to solve more complicated problems. Evidently, success on standard problems is not a reliable indicator of functional understanding.

2. *A coherent conceptual framework is not typically an outcome of traditional instruction: Students need to participate in the process of constructing qualitative models that can help them understand relationships and differences among concepts*

The explanations given by the students in ranking the bulbs in FIGURE 1 indicated that they had failed to integrate the basic electrical concepts into a coherent framework. Rote use of formulas was common. To solve standard circuit problems, skill in mathematical manipulation may suffice. To be able to apply a concept in a variety of contexts, however, students must not only be able to define that concept but also relate it to others. They also need to differentiate that concept from related concepts.

The question was first administered several years ago on an examination in a standard calculus-based course. Lacking a conceptual model on which to base predictions, most students relied on intuition or formulas. About 40% used algebra to find the equivalent resistance of the series and parallel circuits and substituted the result into the formula for the power dissipated in a resistor. However, it is the resistance of a circuit element that affects the power dissipated in that element, not the equivalent resistance of the network of which that element is a part. This error revealed a failure to separate two related concepts: the resistance of an element and the equivalent resistance of a network containing that element.

(a) *Constructing a conceptual model.* A general instructional strategy that we have found useful for helping students relate electrical concepts and distinguish one from another is to engage them actively in the intellectual process of constructing a qualitative model for an electric circuit.[8,9] Development of the model is based on observations of the behavior of batteries and bulbs, preferably through experiments that the students themselves perform.

The students begin the model-building process with two assumptions that appear plausible from their initial observations: (1) a flow (electric current) exists in a complete circuit and (2) bulb brightness indicates the amount of flow. From these assumptions and from observations of the relative brightness of identical bulbs in series and parallel circuits, the students draw inferences about the behavior of bulbs in various configurations. They predict the effect of specified changes on bulb brightness and check their predictions. Using both inductive and deductive reasoning, they formulate the idea that a bulb represents an "obstacle" to the current and recognize that an arrangement of bulbs can be regarded as presenting an "obstacle" that differs from that of a single bulb. After these concepts have been developed, the terms *resistance* and *equivalent resistance* are introduced.

At this point, the students have developed a qualitative model that is sufficient to predict bulb brightness in the relatively complicated circuit shown in FIGURE 2. They can readily determine that the current through bulb E is more than half of the current through the battery. Since bulb A and bulb B each receive half of the current through the battery, they are equally bright but not as bright as bulb E. Bulb C and bulb D each have the same current, but since it is less than half of the current through the battery, they will be dimmer than the others (E > A = B > C = D). Only after students have attained a qualitative understanding of the current do they use the ammeter to make quantitative current measurements.

As the students analyze circuits of increasing complexity, they realize that the model that they have developed thus far is inadequate for predicting the brightness of all the bulbs in some circuits. Model-building continues step-by-step with the introduction of other basic concepts, such as potential difference, power and electrical energy. Gradually, the students construct a conceptual model that enables them to predict and explain the behavior of any electric circuit that contains only resistive elements.

(b) *Quantitative problem-solving.* Experience has shown that emphasis on concept development and model building does not detract from performance on quantitative problems. Many students need explicit instruction on problem solving procedures to develop the requisite skills. However, once equations are introduced, students often avoid thinking of the physics involved. Postponing the use of algebraic formalism until after a qualitative understanding has been developed has proved to be an effective approach. Although less time is available for practice in numerical problem solving, examination results indicate that students who have learned in this way often do better than others on quantitative problems and much better on qualitative questions.[10]

3. *Certain conceptual difficulties are not overcome by traditional instruc-*

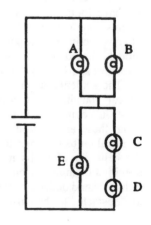

FIGURE 2. Students are asked to rank the bulbs in the circuit according to brightness. The correct response is E > A = B > C = D.

tion. Persistent conceptual difficulties must be explicitly addressed by repeated challenges in more than one context.

Some student difficulties disappear during the normal course of instruction. Others seem to be highly resistant to change. If sufficiently serious, they may preclude meaningful learning, even though performance on quantitative problems may be unaffected. Below we discuss two persistent conceptual difficulties that students often encounter in the study of electric circuits.

In the process of constructing a conceptual model, students often correct several misconceptions about electric circuits. However, we have found that certain common difficulties tend to persist unless explicitly addressed. Two that research has shown to be especially persistent are the belief that current is "used up" in a circuit and the belief that a battery is a constant current source. In courses taught in the standard manner, these misconceptions occur with about the same frequency before and after instruction. Both are illustrated below in the context of FIGURE 1.

First, there is the belief that current is "used up" in a circuit. This is widespread and appears to be intuitive. It is not necessarily a sharply differentiated concept of current that students have in mind. The language many use, however, strongly suggests that they think of current as constantly being produced by the battery and being "used up" by the elements in a circuit. In predicting bulb brightness, many students claimed that one bulb in the series circuit would be brighter than the other. They usually said that "Bulb B is brighter than bulb C because bulb B 'uses up' the current first and bulb C gets the 'left over' current."

The second misconception, a perhaps even more pervasive and persistent one, is the *belief that the battery is a constant current source*—that the current through a battery is always the same. Even good students often do not realize that the current in a circuit depends on the resistance as well as on the battery. The following explanation by a student reflects a conviction that the current in all three circuits in FIGURE 1 is the same:

> A, B and C [are] equal [in brightness] and brighter than D and E, which are equal to each other. The same current *i* goes through A, but in the third circuit the current is divided between D and E.

Deep-seated difficulties, such as those illustrated above, cannot be overcome through assertions by an instructor. Active learning is essential for a significant conceptual change to occur. An instructional strategy that we have found effective for obtaining the necessary intellectual commitment from students is to generate a conceptual conflict and to require them to resolve it. A useful first step is to *elicit* a suspected difficulty by contriving a situation in which students are likely to make a related error. Once the difficulty has been exposed and recognized, the instructor must insist that students *confront* and *resolve* the issue. This sequence of steps does not define a single strategy but a continuum. Below, a variant of this strategy is used to address the misconception that the battery is a constant current source.

Students are asked to compare the current through identical batteries in two circuits: one has a single bulb; the other contains two bulbs in parallel. This task almost always evokes the claim that the current is the same. After this idea has been expressed, the students are asked to note the relative brightness of the bulbs and to consider the implications. The following statement was made by a high school teacher during a workshop when she observed that the bulbs were equally bright and recognized the discrepancy between what she thought would happen and what did happen:

> That would mean that the amount of current from the battery is different in different cases and that doesn't make any sense!

This comment illustrates the kind of reaction that the teaching sequence is meant to generate. In confronting and trying to resolve the conceptual conflict, the teacher was forced to conclude and to begin to believe that the current through a battery is not the same in all circuits.

A single encounter is rarely sufficient to overcome a serious difficulty. Students do not make the same mistakes under all circumstances; the context may be critical. Unless challenged with a variety of situations capable of evoking a given difficulty, students may simply memorize the answer for a particular case. To be able to integrate counterintuitive ideas into a coherent framework, they need time to *apply* the same concepts and reasoning in different contexts, to *reflect* upon these experiences and to *generalize* from them.

4. *Growth in reasoning ability does not usually result from traditional instruction. Scientific reasoning skills must be expressly cultivated.*

An important factor in the difficulties that students have with certain concepts is an inability to do the multi-step qualitative reasoning involved in applying the concept. It is often impossible to separate difficulties with concepts from difficulties with reasoning. An error may be a symptom of an underlying conceptual or reasoning difficulty, or of both.

A failure to think holistically in dealing with compound systems is one kind of reasoning difficulty that may be hard to disentangle from conceptual confusion. For interacting systems, such as elements in an electric circuit, it is impossible to predict the behavior of one without taking into account the effect of the others. Below are two examples of a common tendency to use local sequential reasoning when a holistic approach is needed.

First is a *belief that direction of current and order of elements matter.* In predicting bulb brightness, students often considered only the order of a bulb in an array. Many claimed that the first bulb in a series network was the brightest. This error is consistent with the misconception that current is "used up" and also with improper use of local sequential reasoning. Instead of considering the circuit as a whole, many students focused on one bulb at a time. The conservation of current was an abstraction for which they might be able to write an equation but which they could not apply to a qualitative problem.

Secondly, many students *fail to distinguish between branches connected in parallel across a battery and connected in parallel elsewhere.* Predicting the effects of a change in a circuit requires a more sophisticated level of holistic reasoning. In one task, students were shown a circuit diagram in which a network containing two branches in parallel was connected in series with other bulbs (FIG. 3). The students were asked to predict whether opening the switch would affect the brightness of bulb B. Qualitative reasoning is sufficient to determine that the brightness of bulb B will change.[11] However, many students predicted that the brightness would remain the same because the bulb was part of a parallel combination. In treating the parallel branches as independent, the students were not recognizing the difference between parallel branches connected directly across a battery and parallel branches connected elsewhere. Instead of using qualitative reasoning to check the consistency of their predictions, the students relied on a rule that they had incorrectly memorized.

Traditional instruction does not challenge but tends to reinforce a perception of physics as a collection of facts and formulas.[12] Students often do not recognize the critical role of reasoning in physics, nor do they understand what constitutes an explanation. They need practice in solving qualitative problems and in explaining their reasoning.[13] However, they are unlikely to persevere at developing facility in scientific reasoning unless the course structure, including the examinations, emphasizes the importance of this ability.

5. *Connections among concepts, formal representations, and the real world are often lacking after traditional instruction. Students need explicit practice in interpreting physics formalism and relating it to the real world.*

Students are often unable to relate the concepts and formal representations of physics to one another and to the real world. An inability to interpret equations and diagrams underlies many conceptual and reasoning difficulties. Below are examples from the topics of electric circuits and geometrical optics.

Interpretation of algebraic formalism was a source of difficulty on the task of ranking the bulbs in FIGURE 1. As mentioned earlier, many students confused the resistance of an element with the equivalent resistance of a network or circuit. They had *failed to recognize that the same algebraic symbol is used to represent the resistance of an element and the equivalent resistance of a network.* In their calculations to compare bulb brightness, students often treated the equivalent resistance as a property of an individual bulb rather than as a useful abstraction for finding the total current or potential difference in a branch, network or circuit. The common practice among physicists of representing

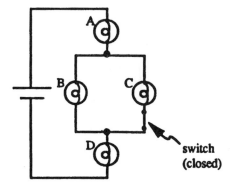

FIGURE 3. Students are asked to predict: (1) the relative brightness of the identical bulbs while the switch is closed (A = D > B = C), and (2) how opening the switch will affect the brightness of each bulb (Bulb B brightens).

resistance and equivalent resistance by the same (or almost the same) symbol contributed to this tendency. To a physicist, each algebraic symbol in an equation represents a well-defined entity. Students, however, may not recognize differences in interpretation that may be associated with the same symbol.

Our investigation of student understanding of the image formed by a converging lens provided another example of the difficulty students often have in relating an algebraic expression to a physical system.[14] Students who had studied the relevant material participated in interviews in which they were shown an object, a thin converging lens and an inverted real image on a screen (FIG. 4). The students were asked what changes would occur if the optical system were altered in certain specified ways. Their responses indicated a *failure to recognize the unique relationship between object and image distances implied by the thin lens formula.*

When asked to predict whether moving the screen toward the lens would change anything on the screen, only 40% of the students recognized that the image would become blurred and disappear. About 45% said that the image would remain clear but its size would change. Although the students had used the thin lens equation (lens maker's equation) to locate an image, many did not recognize that the equation implies that the position of the object uniquely determines the position of the image for a given lens. For every object distance, there is a single image distance.

In addition to difficulty in relating algebraic formalism to the real world, students often cannot interpret the diagrammatic representations used in physics. During interviews on the converging lens tasks, students were encouraged to draw ray diagrams. Many who produced correct diagrams could not relate the information represented to the task at hand.

In one of the tasks, the investigator holds a piece of opaque cardboard above

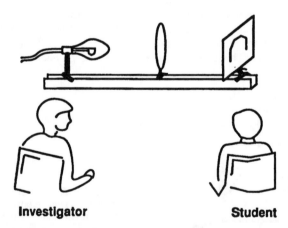

Investigator   **Student**

FIGURE 4. Demonstration for interviews on converging lens tasks. The investigator asks the student what changes would occur if the system were to be altered in certain specified ways.

the lens and asks the student to predict the effect of covering half of the lens. Only about 35% of the students realized that the image would remain intact. The most common immediate response, given by about 55% of the students, was that half of the image would disappear. Some of the ray diagrams drawn by the students reinforced this mistaken intuition.

There was on the part of these students a *failure to recognize that the special rays used in a ray diagram are not necessary for forming an image but are merely convenient for locating its position.*

FIGURE 5 is a ray diagram drawn by a student for the task described above. The student located the image by drawing two rays from the top of the object. One, parallel to the principal axis, is refracted through the focal point; the other through the center of the lens is undeviated. From this essentially correct diagram, the student decided that both rays would be blocked and concluded that the bottom half of the image would be missing. This student was typical of many who did not seem to understand the role of the ray diagram as an algorithm for locating the position of an image.

Although most students who participated in the interviews could solve standard problems, they often were unable to apply the formalism to an actual physical system. Moreover, we found that several factors made no difference in performance: completion of a high school physics course, enrollment in algebra-based or calculus-based physics, participation in the associated laboratory course, or the identity of the instructor.

6. *Teaching by telling is an ineffective mode of instruction for most students. Students must be intellectually active to develop a functional understanding.*

All the examples of student difficulties discussed above share a common feature: the subject matter involved is not difficult. Many instructors expect university students who have studied the relevant material to be able to answer the types of questions that have been illustrated. Yet, in each instance, we found that a large percentage of students could not do the basic reasoning necessary. On certain types of tasks, the outcome did not vary much from one traditionally

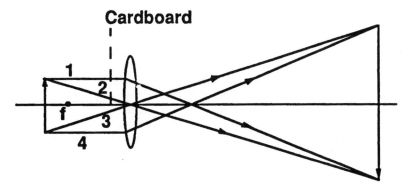

FIGURE 5.   Ray diagram drawn by a student to justify the incorrect prediction that half the image would disappear if half the lens were covered.

taught class to another, nor did it matter when in the course the problems were posed. Enrollment in the associated laboratory course also did not appear to affect the quality of student performance. Moreover, there was no correlation between the success of students and the proficiency of the course instructor as a lecturer.[15]

The difficulties that students have in physics are not usually due to failure of the instructor to present the material correctly and clearly. No matter how lucid the lecture, nor how accomplished the lecturer, meaningful learning will not take place unless students are intellectually active. Those who learn successfully from lectures, textbooks and problem solving do so because they constantly question their own comprehension, confront their difficulties, and persist in trying to resolve them. Most students taking introductory physics do not bring this degree of intellectual independence to their study of the subject.

The common tendency to teach physics by lecturing from the top down runs counter to the way most people learn best. In beginning a new topic, students need to become familiar with the phenomena to be studied, preferably through observation and open-ended investigation. Evidence from research indicates that concept formation is enhanced by "hands-on" experience guided by appropriate questions. Simple demonstrations can also serve as an introduction, provided that students are intellectually active observers. Instead of introducing new concepts or principles by definitions and assertions, the instructor should set up situations that suggest the need for a new concept or the utility of a new principle. Generalization and abstraction should follow, not precede, specific instances in which a concept or principle may apply. Rather than giving direct answers when students ask questions, the instructor should respond with questions that guide students through the reasoning necessary to arrive at their own answers.

Although the traditional lecture and laboratory format has disadvantages, it may be the only mode possible when the number of students is large. Such instruction, however, need not be a passive learning experience. There are several techniques that instructors of large classes can use to promote active participation by students in the learning process.[16]

CONCLUSION: IMPROVING THE MATCH
BETWEEN TEACHING AND LEARNING

Perhaps the most significant contribution that research on learning and teaching can make to the improvement of instruction is to underscore the importance of focusing greater attention on the student. Our experience indicates that success in incorporating a particular topic into a course often depends as much on *how* the material is taught as on *what* is taught. Meaningful learning, which connotes the ability to interpret and use knowledge in situations different from those in which it was initially acquired, requires that students be intellectually engaged. Development of a functional understanding cannot take place unless students themselves go through the reasoning involved in the development and application of concepts. Furthermore, to be able to transfer a reasoning skill learned in one context to another, students need multiple opportunities to use that same skill in different contexts. The entire process requires time. Inevitably, this constraint places a limit on both the breadth of material that can be covered and the pace at which instruction can progress.

ACKNOWLEDGMENT

I would like to thank the other members of the Physics Education Group for important contributions, especially P. Shaffer and J. Valles.

NOTES AND REFERENCES

1. For examples of research and its use for curriculum development on topics not directly related to this paper, see TROWBRIDGE, D. E. & L. C. McDERMOTT. 1980. Investigation of student understanding of the concept of velocity in one dimension. Am. J. Phys. **48:** 1020–1028; TROWBRIDGE, D. E. & L. C. McDERMOTT. Investigation of student understanding of the concept of acceleration in one dimension. 1981. Am. J. Phys. **49:** 242–253; LAWSON, R. A. & L. C. McDERMOTT. 1987. Student understanding of the work-energy and impulse-momentum theorems. Am. J. Phys. **55:** 811–817; McDERMOTT, L. C., M. L. ROSENQUIST & E. H. VAN ZEE. 1987. Student difficulties in connecting graphs and physics: Examples from kinematics. Am. J. Phys. **55:** 503–513; ROSENQUIST, M. L. & L. C. McDERMOTT. 1987. A conceptual approach to teaching kinematics. Am. J. Phys. **55:** 407–415.
2. For an example of a typical text for the calculus-based course, see RESNICK, R., D. HALLIDAY & K. S. KRANE. 1992. *Physics.* Wiley. New York.
3. McDERMOTT, L. C. 1991. What we teach and what is learned—Closing the gap. Am. J. Phys. **59:** 301–315.
4. Discussion in support of this statement appears in: TOBIAS, S. 1990. They're Not Dumb, They're Different. Research Corporation. Tucson, AZ.
5. McDERMOTT, L. C. 1990. A perspective on teacher education in physics and other sciences: The need for special science courses for teachers. Am. J. Phys. **58:** 734–742.
6. The generalizations that appear in this paper also appear in: McDERMOTT, L. C. 1993. How we teach and how students learn—A mismatch? Am. J. Phys. **61:** 295–298.
7. See, for example, ARONS, A. B. 1990. A Guide to Introductory Physics Teaching. Wiley. New York.
8. McDERMOTT, L. C. & P. S. SHAFFER. 1992. Research as a guide for curriculum development: An example from introductory electricity, Part I: Investigation of student understanding. Am. J. Phys. **60:** 994–1003; 1993. Erratum to Part I, Am. J. Phys. **61:** 81. SHAFFER, P. S. & L. C. McDERMOTT. 1992. Research as a guide for curriculum development: An example from introductory electricity, Part II: Design of instructional strategies. Am. J. Phys. **60:** 1003–1013.
9. A similar approach was used by ARONS, A. B. 1977. The Various Language. Oxford. New York, NY.
10. Evidence in support of this statement can be found in Part II of Ref. 8 and E. Mazur (Harvard University). 1992. Improving student understanding in introductory science courses: The peer instruction method. Unpublished.
11. The brightness of bulb B actually increases because the potential difference across its terminals increases when bulb C is removed.
12. Research that supports this point of view is described in HAMMER, D. Epistemological beliefs in introductory physics. Cognition and Instruction. To be published.

13. For a more extensive discussion of the development of reasoning skills, see Ref. 7.
14. GOLDBERG, F. M. & L. C. MCDERMOTT. 1987. An investigation of student understanding of the real image formed by a converging lens or concave mirror. Am. J. Phys. **55:** 108–119.
15. In addition to Refs. 8 and 14, supporting evidence for these statements can be found in HALLOUN, I. A. & D. HESTENES. The initial knowledge state of college physics students. 1985. Am. J. Phys. **53:** 1043–1055; HESTENES, D., M. WELLS & G. SWACKHAMER. 1992. Force concept inventory. Phys. Teach. **30:** 141–158; MAZUR, E. Qualitative vs. quantitative thinking: Are we teaching the right thing? Optics and Photonics News **2:** 38.
16. See, for example, Part II of Ref. 8; HELLER, P., R. KEITH & S. ANDERSON. 1992. Teaching problem solving through cooperative grouping. Part 1: Group versus individual problem solving. Am. J. Phys. **60:** 627–636; HELLER, P. & M. HOLLABAUGH. 1992. Teaching problem solving through cooperative grouping. Part 2: Designing problems and structuring groups. Am. J. Phys. **60:** 637–644; VAN HEUVELEN, A. 1991. Learning to think like a physicist: A review of research-based instructional strategies. Am. J. Phys. **59:** 891–897. The paper by E. Mazur in Ref. 11 provides another example.

What Are the Prerequisites for Success as a Scientific Problem Solver?

JOHN S. EDWARDS

Department of Zoology
University of Washington
Seattle, Washington 98195

INTRODUCTION

Active engagement with classroom learning can be fostered in many ways, among which problem solving makes the most explicit demands on the teacher and on the learner. Like the koans set by the master to the aspiring student of Zen Buddhism, the problem sets the mind into a searching mode in which useful knowledge becomes vital to the solution and in doing so becomes part of the students' awareness. But unlike the long and deep meditation the Zen koan may demand, our life-science students need more readily soluble challenges and the instant positive feedback that comes from success. The art of teaching thus depends in large measure on matching the level of challenge with the students' readiness to learn: active learning requires active teaching. Active teaching, like active learning, is a mental exercise in problem solving, and like any exercise it becomes easier with regular practice—"*Übung macht der meister.*" But practice takes time, it is repetitive, it is an effort, and it can be discouraging when it isn't working. To make matters worse, patterns of contemporary life outside the classroom pull in the opposite direction; the stimuli are diverse and the competition intense.

The college course is a microcosm of these conflicting demands. Competition for time generates a reluctance to seemingly squander it in learning by repetition, by trying again (e.g., "You mean that I should revise the *whole* essay?" or "But I did read the whole chapter through once!"), or by accentuating the teaching of problem-solving skills at the expense of reducing coverage of factual material. Thus the pressures to circumvent dealing with the problems by resorting to a passive, information-rich mode of teaching are many. Among the conflicting pressures to be resolved is the expectation of colleagues that students will emerge from one's class with a certain preparatory body of information that will be brought to bear in their own courses. These problems are exacerbated when the lone proponent of active learning teaches as an island in a sea of passive learning; the student must adapt to different expectations, and other teachers must somehow accommodate to what is perceived as less coverage and inadequate preparation.

What *are* the requisites for success as a scientific problem solver? One answer is simple: success breeds success. There is no better trainer than positive

21

feedback. That is so simple a point that it would scarcely seem to warrant discussion, except that the obstacles to success are many and some deserve attention here.

The first *pre*-requisite to success is, in my view, literally the *prerequisite,* in the curricular catalog sense of the term. Ideally each new course in an optimal sequence stands on the shoulders of those that precede it. Encounters with the facts and with the concepts that give coherence to the relationships between the facts should ideally proceed in an orderly sequence of synthesis. We should, to borrow an example used by Arnold Arons,[1] make sure that students have encountered the concept of inertia in elementary mechanics before coriolis forces are invoked to explain aspects of ocean currents in an oceanography course. Similarly, the basic facts and vocabulary of organic chemistry should precede the challenges of biochemistry, cell biology, and molecular biology. Those are the ideals. Reality, on the other hand, like the larch (as they say on Monty Python), is something completely different. The disparity between real and ideal has many causes, of which some are trivial. For example, students may disclaim previous coverage of material, a disclaimer that can be construed to reflect on the previous teacher rather than the student, and if that means that the material is repeated, so much the better for the tactical advantage of the grade-conscious student who has indeed previously encountered the material. On the other hand, retention is a major variable: things can really have been forgotten. The problem is further complicated by the frequent disparity between published syllabi and the true content of a given course, and by the fact that students come to us via diverse pathways, often as transfer students from institutions of widely varying quality. We seldom work with a homogeneous student population in terms of background, motivation, aptitude, and flexibility.

Another source of disparity between the real and ideal preparation of the biology or zoology major relates to the perennial debate concerning the optimal sequence for introductory material in the teaching of the life sciences. On the one hand, there are those who argue that one should proceed from molecules to ecosystems because that reflects the hierarchy of complexity in living systems. On the other hand there is the view that organisms, their diversity, their inter-actions, their population dynamics, evolution, and extinction are the more appropriate points of departure because they are more immediate to the ex-perience of the student and don't require much more than some basic mathe-matics. As if that issue were not weighty enough, there hovers the ever more urgent challenge of how to constructively deal in the classroom with the crises attending the biological future of planet Earth in the hands of *Homo sapiens,* beside which the finer points of academic biology may be as fiddling while Rome burns, or rearranging the deck chairs on the Titanic.

All this is to say that if students are to be successful as problem solvers, they must be adequately prepared at each successive level, and this requires us to specify our expectations. The Academic Senates of the California Community Colleges, California State Universities, and the University of California have made a laudable move in this direction by setting out what the high school graduate should bring to college biology in a document entitled: "Statement on Preparation in Natural Science Expected of Entering Freshmen." But this is no guarantee of a common background unless it is actively promulgated and acted on; a similar statement in the state of Washington is now gathering dust on an administrator's shelf.

One can hope for broad uniformity in preparation but it is wise to be explicit about what one assumes is brought to a course. For example, at the outset of my 400-level course, I specify material that I assume has been covered in prior courses, and those students with deficiencies are directed to remedial sources.

A second, and equally important requirement for success as a scientific problem solver is to be clear that the process of problem solving in a scientific context is no different from any other context for problem solving. I consider this to be very important, especially in science courses for non-majors, where it is critical to alter the common perception of The Scientist as a priestly class whose mental processing is unique to the initiated. Scientific problem solving is not identical with the Scientific Method, or at least it is not simply the pure hypothetico-deductive sequence that is the standard stuff of the introductory chapters of elementary biology texts. It is a blend of common sense, intuition, analysis, analogy, lateral thinking, trial-and-error—a game of mental natural selection. Scientific problem solving is an extension of everyday problem solving, just as climbing Mount Everest is an extension of climbing stairs.

One reason given for climbing Mount Everest is "because it is there." Perhaps the most cogent reason we can give our students for learning the process of scientific problem solving is also "because the problems are there." The degree of satisfaction in engaging with the material, of building the mental model, and of bringing it to interact with the challenges of the problems set by the course work is probably the surest index of success as a problem solver. One can only hope that this active approach to learning can then be carried on to the level of the greatest problems that the biosphere sets us.

For all the teacher may try, active learning, with or without explicit classroom problem solving, must to a degree rest with a choice by the student to engage with the material. Great problem solvers emerge from educational systems that are based on almost purely rote learning, for example, those of India and China. There are intangibles related to personality and motivation that must play a part in the success of any classroom style.

The third prerequisite for the education of good problem solving students is good problem solving teachers. Again this is a statement of the obvious, but it is important to bear in mind the cyclic nature of the teaching profession: grade school teachers will not actively teach problem solving in biology until we at the colleges prepare the teachers to teach appropriately. If grade school teachers would guide their students to become good problem solvers then (as Ingrith Deyrup-Olsen, a pioneer proponent of active learning, has pointed out) the college teacher could work on the quality of the problems, rather than introducing that way of learning.

A fourth prerequisite in my catalog, but perhaps the first in priority, is what William Bateson, a hundred years ago, in the preface to his monumental book *Materials for the Study of Variation* called "the habit of spontaneous observation." His century-old admonition is highly relevant to our topic, so I quote the context:

From the conditions of the case where very large classes are brought together it becomes necessary that the instruction should be organised, scheduled, and reduced to diagram and system. Facts are valued in proportion as they lend themselves to such orderly treatment; on the rest small store is set. By this method the student learns to think our schemes of Nature sufficient, turning for inspiration to books, and supposing that by following this primer he may master it all. In a specimen he sees what he has been told to see and nothing more, rarely learning the habit of spontaneous observation, the one lesson that the study of Natural History is best fitted to teach. Such a system reacts on the teacher. In time he comes to forget that the caricature of Nature shown to his pupils is like no real thing.[2]

Now, a comment on specifics. I teach two very different courses: human ecology for honors non-majors; and entomology, primarily for senior zoology and biology majors but also for graduate students. The former course assumes little or no science background beyond distantly recalled and often loathed, though sometimes loved, high school courses, while for the entomology course I should be able to assume a basis of elementary biology. The objectives of the two courses are also very different. For the history, sociology, advertising, or English majors one must weave the ideas of science as a way of knowing, its strengths and limits, into the challenge of understanding the processes of the biosphere. The news media bring, at least to peripheral attention, a range of current topics of concern—for example, El Niño and the weather, drought and population crises, global warming, tropical forest and extinctions, radiation hazards, and viruses—all of which can serve as points of departure from the everyday world back to basic principles underlying the phenomena. Here the problem solving component of active learning depends on the teacher's ability to set the scene so that connections can be made.

For the entomology class, the expectations and the products are very different from that of the non-major class and the approach must change accordingly. The candidate for graduate school or the potential Peace Corps entomologist must know something about the structures and the processes that apply to the Class that contains more than 75% of the earth's species, and which are in so many ways different from our own minority group, the vertebrates. Here evolution provides the context for problem solving; we can consider the arthropods and the vertebrates as alternative evolutionary solutions to the challenges of terrestrial life. Then a host of intriguing problems arise: how can one do without red blood cells, without lungs, without kidneys? The questions often have the salutary effect of sending the puzzled student back to a text on vertebrate biology to become aware, perhaps for the first time, of how our skin works, and then how it differs from the integument of an insect with its elegant mechanisms for waterproofing and providing structural support. In the lab, the process of taxonomic identification through dichotomous keys is a very different exercise. It can be classically dull, but it is again an activity in which students, working in pairs or small groups, focus on sharply-defined problem solving, where practice certainly has quick rewards in ease of decision making.

The field trip can be a rolling opportunity to set problems, from taxonomic to ecological, and from developmental to ethological, in their natural context.

The common element that runs through the two very different classes discussed above, for the non-major and for the senior in zoology, is the cultivation of questions rather than the dispensing of data. For both courses, testing is either take-home or open-notes (*not* open book—there is a big difference), and the accent is on using data rather than remembering them, but it is truly surprising how much data is remembered as a result!

THE PREREQUISITES FOR SUCCESSFUL PROBLEM SOLVING: THE RESULTS OF AN OPEN FORUM

The foregoing presents the perspective I brought to the workshop. It is evident that I saw the issue in terms of appropriate preparation and expectation; I took the students' active engagement in the enterprise as a given. Somewhat to my surprise a complementary perspective emerged from a poll of workshop participants taken at the outset of our discussion. The poll revealed a complementary view of the prerequisites for problem solving in the classroom that emphasized personal characteristics of the student. Self-confidence, curiosity, or motivation were the attributes chosen by about half of the participants (TABLE 1). One-third of them mentioned personal skills, while a mere 5% cited curricular mastery, of physics or chemistry for example. After an hour of vigorous discussion in open forum format, the participants were again polled with the same question. Again over half of the participants' responses listed curiosity, motivation or self-confidence as the key ingredients, while a quarter

TABLE 1. Results of Instant Poll of Workshop Participants in Which They were Asked to Identify the Most Significant Factor Promoting Successful Problem Solving in the Classroom.

Before Discussion		After Discussion	
Self-confidence	16	Curiosity	15
Curiosity	13	Motivation	14
Motivation	6	Self-confidence	9
Interest in learning	6	Teacher attitude	6
Ability to do critical observation	6	Ability to problem-solve	6
Independent thinking	4	Hypothesis formation	3
Ability to communicate	4	Background preparation	3
Elementary chemistry/physics/biology	3	Communication skills	3
Comfort with ambiguity	2	Reasoning skills	2
Quantitative skills	2	Observation skills	2
Reasoning ability	3	Quantitative skills	1
Language skills	2	Provision of appropriate context	1
Biodiversity data	1	Positive reinforcement	1
Ability to visualize	1		
Positive reinforcement	1		
Don't know	1		

chose skills such as reasoning, quantitative ability, or communication. But perhaps perceptions of the question did change a little during the discussion, for teacher attitude, course design, and preparation accounted for 20% of choices in the second poll.

CONCLUSIONS

The prerequisites for success as a problem solver are no different from those of problem solving in any other context, to the extent that they encompass the complementary qualities of preparedness and motivation. Self-confidence, curiosity, motivation, and interest provide for the resilience to rebound from unproductive leads and the patience to try again. These qualities promote passive learning also, but they come into play in more explicit ways in an active learning context. Success breeds success; the sense of achievement in active learning can be addictive (without being harmful to the health, as far as we know). It depends on the creation of an appropriate milieu, and a critical part of that milieu is the set of skills that is carried forward from topic to topic and from course to course. Success is to a large degree dependent on having the appropriate factual background for a given course. That is not to deny the possibility that in skilled hands a naive student can be guided to great heights, but to emphasize the necessary conditions for the average student in classes ranging from introductory biology to advanced clinical or research training.

Just what the ideal sequence of material for active learning in biological sciences might be is open to debate. Differing opinions on the best way to open up the interwoven network of the phenomena we call life into a linear sequence may never be resolved.

The information explosion compounds the challenge of what and how to teach, as does the need to confront the implications of human impact on the biosphere. One can only hope that the cultivation of the capacity for problem solving, for generalizing, and for maintaining an active classroom engagement with the life sciences at all levels will produce citizens who are prepared to face the most complex contemporary challenges in all problem solving: the crises facing the biological health of the planet Earth.

REFERENCES

1. ARONS, A. B. 1983. Achieving wider scientific literacy. Daedalus **112:** 91–112.
2. BATESON, W. 1894. Materials for the Study of Variation. Macmillan. London.

Why Am I Teaching This Course?
Setting Educational Objectives
for Course Activities[a]

HAROLD I. MODELL[b]

National Resource for Computers in Life Science Education
Seattle, Washington 98115

Why am I teaching this course? This is a question that is seldom asked because the answer seems all too obvious. I am teaching this course because, in one way or another, it falls within my job description. This certainly answers one reading of the question—why am *I* teaching this course? It does not, however, address another interpretation of the question. That is, *why* am I teaching this course? What is my purpose for or what do I intend to accomplish by teaching this course? Certainly these questions are asked when designing a curriculum. Lecture courses are included in the curriculum as a forum to make students aware of a body of information. A need to provide students with an opportunity to practice observation and measurement skills necessary for engaging in scientific enquiry leads to including a laboratory course in the curriculum.

Once a course has been established, however, faculty appear to stop asking these questions. They seldom establish teaching goals for the classroom. This is puzzling because setting goals is an integral part of nearly all of the science community's other academic endeavors. Experiments in the research laboratory are designed to test specific hypotheses, and those experiments are designed so that they offer a high probability of acquiring appropriate data. Hence, the goal of testing the hypothesis drives the design of the experiment. In the same way, establishing teaching goals drives the design of the classroom activities that will take place.

When one attends lectures in similar courses offered by different faculty or at different institutions, the experience is remarkably similar. The lecturer stands in front of the class and, often with a variety of visual aids, speaks to the class. Occasionally, the lecturer may ask a question, but it is generally in the form of a rhetorical question, and the lecturer does not seek answers from the class. When the faculty delivering those lectures are persuaded to articulate the goals of their teaching efforts, however, an interesting picture develops. For some faculty, the goal is to *tell* the students all they need to know about a given topic. For others, the goal is to *help their students understand* their area of expertise. Still others intend to *get their students to think* about the science in which they

[a]This work was funded in part by NIH Grant 1R43 DK44064-01

[b]Address for correspondence: Harold I. Modell, Ph.D., NRCLSE, P.O. Box 51187, Seattle, Washington 98115.

are involved. Certainly, instructors whose goal it is to tell the students all they need to know have achieved their teaching goals. Their goal relates to their performance, not the students'. These faculty decide what information needs to be disseminated, and they disseminate it.

To achieve the goals of those instructors who want to help their students understand or get their students to think requires involvement by the students. The task is no longer to simply present information. The manner in which the information is presented may be important, and how the students respond to the information becomes a concern. If these instructors do not interact with their students, they have no way of knowing if their efforts have been productive. They have not asked themselves what classroom activities will best help them achieve their goals for the class. If we are to improve the educational process, we must consider what we are trying to accomplish in the classroom on a daily basis and then choose classroom activities that will provide the greatest chance of achieving those goals.

An example of the value of setting teaching objectives is illustrated by the current "controversy" surrounding the use of live animal preparations in student laboratories. Many institutions are rescheduling laboratory time originally devoted to live preparations with activities that involve computer simulations. In conversation with faculty seeking new laboratory activities, one repeatedly hears the phrase "substitutes or alternatives for existing animal laboratories." The implication is that these technological approaches can provide the same experience that the live preparation laboratories provided. In fact, this is not the case. How well this rescheduling meets the needs of the curriculum depends on the educational goals of the specific laboratory time.

From an educational standpoint, the issue is not whether to use live preparations or computer simulations. The issue is defining the educational goals for the class time. Having established these goals, the decision becomes obvious. If the goal is to demonstrate basic physiological principles with which the students can build and utilize conceptual models of physiological systems, the computer model most likely provides a better vehicle than the live preparations. If, on the other hand, the goal is to provide students with a better understanding of the complexity of a living system or give students a first-hand experience with living tissue, rescheduling the time for a computer simulation is counterproductive. In some cases, some combination of the two may lead to the highest probability of success. When educational objectives are taken into account, there is no controversy. The activity chosen, in this case, live animal preparation or computer program, is the one that offers the best chance of achieving the educational goals.[1]

Setting teaching goals for the classroom is not a difficult task. All that is involved is asking oneself, "What do I want to accomplish in the classroom?" The key is that this is a conscious act just as designing an experiment in the laboratory is a conscious act. Having established a goal, the next step is to choose activities that will provide the greatest chance of reaching those goals, just as when designing an experiment, each step is taken to provide data on the appropriate variables. The process easily becomes a habit that directs one's teaching effort just as it directs one's scientific enquiry. The following scenarios illustrate how establishing teaching goals helps define classroom activities at a variety of levels.

SCENARIO 1

Background:

The class setting is a "lecture hall" and the topic of the day is an introduction to renal physiology. In the sequence of course topics, renal physiology is taught after several other areas (e.g., muscle, cardiovascular, and respiratory physiology).

Teaching goals:

The instructor has two main teaching objectives. The first is to present an overview of renal function. The second is to have students generate a list of concepts with which they are familiar from their earlier experience in physiology and that they expect to find applied to the renal system.

Analysis of the teaching goals:

The instructor can achieve the first goal by telling the class what the kidney does and what processes are involved in the formation of urine. In that case, the students would only participate by taking lecture notes. This would not meet the second goal. The instructor wants the students to draw upon their past experience and, as a group, develop a list of concepts that they will look for in the subsequent days' discussions. Thus, the students must interact with, at least, the instructor and, preferably, also with fellow students. The role of the instructor in this class session becomes that of a facilitator rather than a lecturer.

Approach in the classroom:

The session begins with the instructor asking the class what they know about the function of the kidney. Elicited responses include urine formation, "cleansing" of blood, perhaps sodium and water balance, and, perhaps, a role in blood pressure regulation. From these responses, the instructor establishes that plasma is filtered, water and solutes are reabsorbed, and some substances are secreted. At this point, the instructor may also elect to provide an overview of the anatomy of the nephron. The next step to achieving the teaching goal is to focus on each of the processes involved in urine formation (i.e., filtration, reabsorption, secretion) and ask the students what factors they expect to find influencing each of these processes. In response, the students review Starling forces governing water movement at the capillary, general aspects of active transport, the sodium-postassium-ATPase pump, carrier-mediated facilitated diffusion, and passive diffusion. In addition, they establish a set of expectations for the physiological mechanisms at work in the nephron.

Comment:

In this scenario, the instructor felt that by having the students generate a list of concepts that they thought they would encounter in renal physiology, they would recognize that much of the material that would serve as the focus for subsequent sessions was not new to them. The intent, then, was to help students extend their current conceptual framework to a new area. To achieve the goal, it was necessary for the instructor to modify his role in the classroom from a disseminator of information to a facilitator of discussion. The resulting classroom activities reflected this change.

SCENARIO 2

Background:

A faculty member is preparing a series of lectures dealing with the regulation of cardiac output and arterial blood pressure. Student feedback in previous years has indicated that, during these lectures, the students feel as if considerable time is spent focusing on details, and they are not able to see where these details fit into "the big picture." In previous years, the instructor has provided students with a syllabus that includes a list of objectives for each lecture. The phrasing of these objectives was consistent with what has become standard practice in providing learning objectives. That is, they were stated in the form of a series of tasks (e.g., define these words, describe this process, etc.). Conversations with students after each lecture left the instructor with the impression that the objectives, as provided, were not helpful to the student during the lecture period.

Teaching goals:

In response to the feedback and impressions from previous years, the instructor has two new teaching objectives for this series of lectures. The first is to provide a more global framework so that students can better understand where the material in each lecture fits within the overall scheme of cardiovascular regulation. The second new goal is to present the learning objectives in a manner that will be helpful to students during the lecture as well as when they are studying for the test.

Analysis of the teaching goals:

The goal of helping students understand how the topic of the day fits into the general scheme of cardiovascular regulation could be accomplished by providing the students with a global frame of reference that would serve as the starting point and summary point of each lecture. The second goal could be accomplished by including the learning objectives as part of the introduction to the lecture. In addition, restating the objectives in the form of questions aimed at understanding the mechanisms to be discussed would help the students view the information presented in the lecture as answers to specific questions rather than a collection of facts. For example, an objective dealing with the baroreceptor reflex that was originally stated as "understand[ing] the reflex effects of arterial baroreceptor stimulation on heart rate, peripheral resistance, and blood pressure" would be restated as "what is the mechanism by which the baroreceptor reflex controls arterial blood pressure?"

Approach in the classroom:

To achieve the stated goals, the instructor prepared new visual aids for use at the beginning and end of the lecture. The first visual aid was a schematic diagram illustrating the interaction of the factors responsible for cardiovascular regulation. This slide was used as the initial slide of the lecture. The instructor first outlined briefly the factors involved in cardiovascular regulation and then told the students which factors would serve as the focus for the current lecture. To address how the specific factors would be approached, the instructor presented the restated objectives (now in the form of questions) for the day. At the end of the lecture, the instructor used the objective questions to summarize and review the key points in the lecture, and she reviewed the initial slide to remind students where the day's material fit within the global picture and to provide a preview of the next day's lecture material.

Comment:

Unlike the first scenario in which the teaching goals dictated the type of classroom interaction, the goals in this scenario focus on one aspect of the instructor's lecture. The goal pointed to two changes in the visual aids used, and to changes in presentation style that took only a few minutes of lecture time. These small changes potentially impacted the effectiveness of the lecture significantly.

SCENARIO 3

Background:

A laboratory course paralleled the lecture course described in Scenario 2 to provide students with an opportunity to better relate what they learned in lecture to living systems. The traditional experiment involving cardiovascular regulation in the dog was run to reinforce the information presented in the lectures dealing with blood pressure regulation. Because of the faculty-student ratio, it was not possible for a faculty member to be present with each laboratory group of 4–6 students during the entire experiment. As a result, students had to rely on the written protocol for direction during the experiment. Observations by the faculty indicated that although the students went through the experiment, they did not derive full benefit from it because they did not think about what they were doing and seeing. They seemed to perform the appropriate maneuvers and make observations, but they did not perform any analysis on the data nor did they discuss the implications of their data as they collected it. Thus, if they deviated from the prescribed protocol, they were not necessarily aware of it, and, as a result, when they tried to analyze their data at the end of the experiment, they were apt to draw erroneous conclusions.

Teaching goals:

The faculty's goal with respect to this and the other laboratory exercises in the course was to help students to think about the physiological system as they were running the experiment and consider their data as they obtained it.

Analysis of the teaching goals:

Perhaps the best way to achieve the goal for this laboratory course would have been for a faculty member to work with each small group of students to prompt discussion of the data as it was being obtained. Since the faculty/student ratio precluded this, some direction had to be provided for the times when faculty were not with a lab group. The key to providing this direction was redesigning the written protocol given to the students.

Approach in the classroom:

The original protocol was written as a series of "to do" instructions. The students were instructed to perform a maneuver (e.g., inject acetylcholine via the femoral vein), record their observations, perform another maneuver (e.g., inject epinephrine via the femoral vein), record their observation, etc. The last section of the protocol presented a number of questions relating to the data.

The revised protocol encouraged the students to think about what they were about to do, predict what they thought would happen, compare their data with their predictions, and explain any discrepancies (was the "problem" with their mental models, with the experimental design, or with their observations?). The following excerpt illustrates the form of the revised protocol.

Our first test substance will be acetylcholine (ACh). What portion of the autonomic nervous system will we be mimicking? ACh stimulates muscarinic receptors. When we inject the ACh, what responses do you predict we should see? Inject 5 micrograms/Kg into the femoral vein. What happened to heart rate? Is this what you predicted? What happened to arterial blood pressure? Is this what you predicted? What caused the change in arterial blood pressure?[2]

By asking the students relevant questions as they did the experiment, the new protocol continually focused student attention on the physiology being examined.

Comment:

If the faculty involved in this scenario had been polled to determine the purpose of the laboratories, the response would have reflected the stated teaching goals. However, in the initial design of the laboratory exercise and accompanying protocol, these goals were not articulated. As a result, a traditional protocol was written that did not meet the faculty's intent. By articulating the goals and analyzing the existing classroom activities, it became clear that the protocol, as written, did not foster the learning experience that was intended. The revision of this one component offered the potential of markedly changing the learning environment experienced by the students.

SCENARIO 4

Background:

The setting for this scenario is a class of 100 students learning respiratory physiology. The focus for day's session is the elastic properties of the lung, chest wall, and total respiratory system. Historically, when considering the interaction between lung and chest wall mechanics, students understand that when the respiratory system is at rest (i.e., end-expiration), the recoil of the lung and chest wall are pulling in opposite directions and that the volume of the system reflects the balance between these two forces. Students have a difficult time, however, accepting that, at this point, intrapleural pressure is subatmospheric.

Teaching objectives:

The instructor has several teaching objectives for this session. The first goal is to foster an active learning environment. The second goal is to have students realize that the concepts used to describe the elastic properties of the respiratory system apply to all elastic structures. Next, he wants the students to gain an appreciation for what is meant by elastic recoil and recoil pressure. The final goal is to help the students *discover* that, when the respiratory system is at rest, the intrapleural pressure must be subatmospheric.

Analysis of the teaching goals:

If the classroom is to be an active learning environment, the students must engage in the process of building their own mental models of, in this case, an elastic structure.[3] One approach to achieving the second and third goals is to have each student work with an elastic structure with which they are familiar and use that structure as a model of the components of the respiratory system. In this way, each student personally manipulates the model, resulting in a more intimate experience than listening to a lecture or viewing a demonstration. A suitable model in this case is a common balloon. To achieve the final goal, the students must extend their model to the components of the respiratory system, and, drawing on their own experience, determine what the intrapleural pressure should be when the respiratory system is at rest.

Approach in the classroom:

Each student was given a balloon at the beginning of class. After a brief introduction about elastic structures, the students were told to make the volume of the balloon bigger and to hold it at the new volume with their fingers. The instructor then asked the class what they had to do to displace the balloon from its resting volume (i.e., where transmural pressure is zero). Through this and the subsequent dialog, the students recognized that a positive transmural pressure is necessary to oppose the balloon's recoil and keep the volume greater than its resting volume. Furthermore, by holding the balloon at the inflated volume, the students can feel the pressure generated by the recoil of the balloon.

After running several other experiments with the balloon, the instructor presented the class with schematic representations of various elastic structures with the pressures on the inside and outside of the structures indicated. For each of these visuals, the students were asked to indicate by a show of hands whether the structure was greater than or less than its resting volume. The instructor then carried the discussion a step further to consider two elastic structures, each with a different resting volume, coupled together to form a third elastic structure (i.e., the lung and chest wall to form the total respiratory system). The students then determined what the pressures on the inside and outside of the lung and chest wall must be under the conditions where the total respiratory system is at rest (i.e., no air flow and respiratory muscles relaxed).

Through this exercise, these students reasoned from their own mental models, that if, in the intact respiratory system at functional residual capacity (i.e., the resting volume of the system), the lung is greater than its unstressed volume and the chest wall is smaller than its unstressed volume, the intrapleural pressure must be subatmospheric.

Comment:

The teaching goals in this scenario required the instructor to establish an active learning environment in the classroom. Although the students in Scenario

1 were also engaged in an active learning process, the role of the instructor in this scenario was very different from that in the earlier scenario. In the earlier situation, the instructor facilitated a student-directed discussion in which existing mental models were reviewed to speculate on the application of those models to a new area of focus. In this scenario, the instructor directed the session so that the class engaged in a series of exercises designed to help students extend their current mental models to a new area of focus.

CONCLUSION

Because designing materials and activities for the classroom should follow the same process that determines activities in the research laboratory, the teacher should view the classroom as his or her educational laboratory. Hence, teaching goals (hypotheses) should be articulated, necessary materials and activities (experimental methods) that will give the best chance of success should be developed, and the class should be conducted with those goals in mind (the experiment should be run). We have not discussed the critical final steps in the process, that of assessment (data acquisition) and analysis. These steps must be included if we are to make progress in our collective goal of helping students to learn, and they are addressed elsewhere in this volume by Angelo.[4] Establishing educational objectives should form the basis of all that we do in the curriculum, from setting the overall program to helping students understand the message contained in a single slide. Educational objectives must also be taken into consideration when we design examinations and other forms of assessment. The bottom line is that if we expect to improve the educational process, we, as educators, must consciously decide what we want to accomplish and then do all we can to ensure that we achieve those goals.

REFERENCES

1. MODELL, H. I. 1989. Can technology replace live preparations in student laboratories? Am. J. Physiol. **256** (Adv. Physiol. Educ. **1**): S18–S20.
2. MODELL, H. I. 1991. Designing protocols for student laboratories. Computers in Life Sci. Educ. **8**: 91–94.
3. MODELL, H. I. & J. A. MICHAEL. 1993. Promoting active learning in the life science classroom: Defining the issues. Ann. N.Y. Acad. Sci. This volume.
4. ANGELO, T. A. 1993. Promoting active learning through classroom assessment. Ann. N.Y. Acad. Sci. This volume.

Teaching Problem Solving in Small Groups[a]

JOEL A. MICHAEL

Department of Physiology
Rush Medical College
Chicago, Illinois 60612

INTRODUCTION

American education has, in general, failed to prepare students to be active learners and has failed to help them to become problem solvers.[1] If this is to be remedied, one possible response is to reexamine the ways in which we as life science teachers make use of the traditional small group sessions which are frequently scheduled in parallel with lecture presentations.

The focus of this essay will be on how to create active, small group experiences to assist students to learn to solve problems in the life sciences. After defining the educational objectives for such experiences as precisely as possible, I will describe a number of different types of small group sessions, and then discuss the issues that must be addressed in order to implement such sessions successfully.

WHAT IS MEANT BY ACTIVE LEARNING?

It is easy to describe the most common form of passive learning: students sitting in a lecture hall listening to a speaker and perhaps attempting to transcribe onto paper what is being heard. Passive learning involves memory storage and little else. Active learning, on the other hand, occurs when students engage additional cognitive processes while confronting the information being acquired (whether visually, orally, or tactilely),[2,3] relating the new information to the existing knowledge base, generating questions about the new information, attempting to validate already generated hypotheses with the new information, or using the new information to solve problems. Active learning is known to lead to better retention, better retrieval, and, in general, a better ability to use the acquired information in other contexts.[3]

Active learning is not something that is done *for* students; it is something that learners do for themselves. Active learning *can* occur in front of a textbook or in the lecture hall, although it rarely does so spontaneously. One reason for this is that the processes that support students' active learning are skills that are

[a]Portions of this work have been supported by the Cognitive Science Program, Office of Naval Research, under Grant N00014-91-J-1622, Grant Authority Identification Number AA1711319, to Rush Medical College.

rarely taught and hence rarely practiced. Small group sessions represent one learning environment in which these skills can be fostered in a direct manner and with immediate reinforcement from the teacher.

WHAT IS PROBLEM SOLVING?

What exactly is meant by problem solving? In some sense it simply refers to what must be done when the answer to a question or problem cannot simply be retrieved from memory. That is, relevant information must be retrieved from memory (or some external source) and then *something must be done with that information* (combine it, compare or contrast it, integrate the pieces in a new whole, etc.) in order to arrive at a state that represents a solution to the problem.[4]

In physiology, or any of the life sciences, we generally ask students to carry out two quite different kinds of problem solving. We may ask them to carry out numerical calculations to determine the value of cardiac output, renal clearance, alveolar partial pressure of carbon dioxide, etc. These quantitative problems are similar to problems the students have encountered in the past in physics, chemistry, or algebra. A different kind of problem solving is required when students are asked to *predict* the behavior of a system that has been perturbed, or to *explain* the behavior of a system that has been disturbed. This kind of problem requires students to reason about the qualitative, causal relationships between the components of the system being considered, a skill that has probably rarely been exercised in the past. An equivalent exercise is to design an experiment to test an hypothesis about some biological phenomenon; here both qualitative and quantitative problem solving may be required.

Problem solving, then, requires both some fund of knowledge and the skills required to use this knowledge to achieve some desired end. While students, at every educational level, have been well prepared as memorizers, few of them have had the opportunity to develop their skills as problem solvers. This is the challenge for small group sessions.

THE EDUCATIONAL OBJECTIVE
OF SMALL GROUP SESSIONS

Put in most global terms, the educational objective of small group sessions is to give each individual student an opportunity to practice the application of knowledge to the solving of problems in a setting in which the instructor can evaluate the student's performance and provide appropriate, personalized feedback about his or her performance. Note that such sessions may have other objectives of equal importance, and may have a variety of different sub-goals. I will deal with some of these below when I discuss specific types of small group sessions.

Although the goal I have defined is addressed to the needs of the *individual* student, this does not mean that the ultimately effective small group session is a teacher and a student at opposite sides of a desk. On the contrary, there is considerable reason to believe that some of the most valuable learning experiences arise from the interaction of students with each other,[5] and the significance of this will also be discussed below. I will be discussing group sessions in which the numbers of students vary from 3 to 4 to perhaps 20 to 30, but there is no reason why ingenuity can not be used to apply the ideas to be presented here to still larger groups. *In the end, it is not the number of students involved that is important but what it is the instructor has arranged for them to do that will determine the learning outcomes.*

There are at least two important consequences that arise from the acceptance of the above educational objective that need to be mentioned. The first is that a small group session must aim at providing students with opportunities for active and interactive learning, as opposed to the kind of passive learning typified by a lecture. This, in turn, requires a certain kind of teaching behavior from instructors that may be quite different from what is usually expected of them. Second, small group sessions are not usually the setting in which students are expected to learn *new* knowledge (lectures and textbooks are more appropriate for that role), rather, they are the setting in which students will learn to integrate and use the knowledge that they have already acquired.

TYPES OF SMALL GROUP SESSIONS

As teachers of physiology, or any of the life sciences, we have all had some experience with two broad types of small group sessions: laboratory and discussion sessions. *Laboratory sessions* are characterized by the opportunities they provide for students to interact in some direct, more or less hands-on, way with the biological systems about which they were learning. It is thought that such direct, active experience will lead to integration of knowledge, and the ability to apply that knowledge to solving problems (to explain phenomena, make predictions). *Discussion sessions* have traditionally been experiences in which students are given an opportunity to consider and talk through the solutions to problems presented to them in some format. In both types of sessions it was expected that the instructors (whether faculty or teaching assistants) will provide the feedback necessary to facilitate learning.

I will not dwell on the great disparity between objectives and reality that all too often is present in such small group sessions: labs that are exercises in rote, unthinking carrying out of experimental protocols followed by mindless, formulaic processing of data, or discussion sessions that are nothing more than passive exercises in transcribing problem solutions from the blackboard to a notebook. Instead, I will attempt to describe how to make these sessions the active learning experiences we want them to be.

It is neither necessary nor appropriate here to describe in detail all of the possible types of laboratory and discussion groups. However, it will be useful to at least list some of the more common types that we may find on, or want to put on, our educational menus.

Laboratory Sessions

There are at least four different kinds of laboratory experiences that we provide for our students. These are:

- "wet" labs, whatever the biological preparation might be,
- human labs, in which students serve as the experimental preparation,
- computer simulated labs, in which the experiment is carried out solely with some kind of hardware system (computer, interactive video); and
- labs in which students interact with physical or chemical models relevant to the understanding of living systems.

In any such laboratory settings students are expected to carry out some experimental protocol (whether self-generated or provided by the instructor) and then do something with the results that are obtained. This may consist of writing a laboratory report, answering a series of questions, or simply preparing to be tested on an exam. The role of the instructor in such a setting is to assist, when needed, in the conduct of the experiment, to answer questions generated by the students, and to stimulate, in any appropriate manner, student thinking about the experience.

Discussion Sessions

The variety of types of discussion sessions is at least as great as the variety in laboratories, but such sessions seem to carry a more diverse set of labels (sections, tutorials, workshops, discussion groups, problem solving groups). Here then is a list of some of the kinds of discussion sessions that are commonly encountered:

- teaching-assistant–run sections in which lecture material and/or home-work assignments are reviewed;
- laboratory review sessions in which the results of recently completed experiments are discussed;
- sessions specifically devoted to learning to solve problems (whether quantitative, pathophysiological, clinical); and
- small group problem solving sessions making up a problem-based course or curriculum.

In all such discussion sessions it is generally understood that student participation is to be elicited to as great an extent as possible, that student problem solving performance will be critiqued, and that the instructor will model the problem solving processes being carried out when necessary.

EDUCATIONAL PLANNING FOR SUCCESSFUL SMALL GROUP SESSIONS

The implementation of successful small group sessions in which active learning to solve problems occurs requires the consideration of a large number of issues. I will begin by listing some of these issues and will then return to discuss each of them in more detail:

1. the overall course objectives;
2. the "structure" of the course;
3. the type of small group being planned;
4. the educational objectives for such sessions;
5. the learning resources that will be available for the session;
6. the manner in which the session will be conducted;
7. the role or function of the instructor in each session; and
8. the manner in which student performance will be assessed.

What Are the Overall Educational Objectives for the Course that I am Teaching?

Regardless of the educational level at which we teach, this is perhaps the single most important question we must ask when we plan any aspect of our course. We must define the *knowledge base* (facts, concepts, principles, terminology, etc.), the *problem solving skills* (solving quantitative problems, predicting system responses, designing experiments), and the other *special skills* (use of lab instrumentation, experimental manipulations, etc.) that we want the students to acquire or master. These decisions will largely determine what you want to achieve in small groups sessions (if any) that you plan for your course.

How Are You Teaching This Course? What Is the Structure of the Course?

The issues to be confronted here are many. Is this predominately a lecture course? Or perhaps predominately a laboratory course? How much time do you have? How much contact time is available for each student? How many students are involved? How many instructors are available to conduct small group sessions? When in the sequence of things can you schedule small group sessions? How do you carry out student assessments in this course? The answers to these questions represent the constraints within which you must operate as you plan small group sessions of any kind.

What Type of Small Group Sessions Are You Planning to Schedule?

Although many of the issues to be considered are quite general, it is clear that laboratory sessions and discussion groups raise different questions for the instructor to answer.

If you are planning for laboratory sessions you must decide what kind of exercise will best meet your educational objectives. To meet some objectives (learning experimental methodologies, learning first hand the requirements of working on living tissue) it is essential that traditional "wet labs" be used with the appropriate biological preparation. Other objectives can be achieved equally well with traditional "wet labs" or with human experiments, and local constraints (budget, space, resources, etc.) will determine which kind of approach can be employed. In still other circumstances the use of simulated experiments may produce the best learning outcomes.

The choice of what kind of small group session to incorporate in your course is no less determined by both your educational objectives and your local constraints. If you are teaching medical or human physiology you may want to organize problem solving sessions in which students confront human pathophysiology problems, while if you are teaching an undergraduate comparative physiology course you may want students to analyze possible adaptations to different environmental niches.

What Are the Educational Objectives for the Small Group Session You Are Planning?

I have suggested very strongly that one objective for *all* small group sessions ought to be the development of problem solving skills by the students. If we take this as a given, there are nevertheless a number of other possible objectives for each type of small group session that has been discussed.

Although small group sessions are rarely intended to be the forum for the presentation of (lecturing on) new material, they are an appropriate setting in which students can be encouraged to discover for themselves what new information they need to acquire in order to master some topic or solve some problem. Problem-based courses[6] or a problem-based learning curriculum[7,8] use small group sessions to solve problems and in the course of solving problems to generate learning issues for later study. This, then, represents another possible objective for small group sessions.

In many cases, small group sessions are intended as a setting in which students can apply their knowledge and problem solving skills to particular kinds of problems. For example, sessions might be devoted to dealing with specific clinical problems or they might involve a focus on experimental design. The ability to apply what is learned from textbooks and/or lectures in a specific problem solving context then becomes another objective.

In planning laboratory sessions there are always decisions to be made about the importance of mastering the use of the experimental techniques being employed, whether instrumentation or surgical, etc. Are students to carry out an experiment described in great detail for them, design an experiment on their own, or some combination of these approaches?

What Resources Will Be Made Available to Students in the Small Group Sessions?

Obviously, to conduct laboratory sessions one must be able to provide the resources required for such activities: animals, instrumentation, chemicals and supplies, and space. It is, however, equally important that the instructor make available to the students some material defining the exercise to be carried out. This may range from the brief description of a question to be addressed and list of the equipment available for carrying out an experiment, to a complete description of the experimental protocol to be pursued. As is always the case, the decision of where along this continuum to operate must be determined by the objectives you have formulated for this experience.

In addition to the physical resources required for a laboratory session and some description of the exercise, it is equally important that the instructor provide the context or stimulus that will make the session an active learning experience. This can be accomplished in a variety of ways, but it must be done explicitly or it is not likely to happen at all. An instructor circulating among the laboratory stations and asking thought-provoking questions can be the most effective means of keeping the students' heads as busy as their hands. Problem solving questions (requiring application and integration of information, not just recall of facts) scattered throughout the laboratory protocol (and to be answered) can serve a similar function. The goal, though, is active thinking *while the laboratory exercise is being carried out.* Student promises that they will think about what it all means while they write up the experiment back in their dorm room are generally quite empty.

For discussion sessions of any kind the only resource that is absolutely required is a set of problems to be solved. These must, of course, be carefully formulated to meet the educational objectives of the sessions, both in terms of their content (what phenomena are being discussed) and the problem solving skills to be mastered. The choice of problems to be presented to the students must take into consideration the degree of difficulty that is appropriate (and the rate at which problems become more difficult), the kinds of problems used (pathophysiological, clinical, experimental, etc.), and the time available in your session for solving or discussing the problem.

How Will the Small Group Sessions Be Conducted?

Given that small group sessions are to be the most active possible learning experiences for the students, there are a number of ways of reaching that goal. Students can be asked to work cooperatively in groups[9,10] or they can be asked to work individually. Individual students, or groups of students, can be given the responsibility for "publicly" presenting solutions to the problems, with the instructor intervening only when necessary. Problems can be assigned ahead of time and worked on in advance, or they may be confronted for the first time in the small group session. Answers to assigned problems, or some written product, may have to be handed in for grading. Alternatively, short quizzes can be conducted during the sessions, or course exams may contain examples of the problems that students are expected to learn to solve. Decisions about such features of the small group experience are as applicable to laboratory sessions as they are to discussion groups.

What Role Should the Instructor
Assume in Each Session?

If the goal of small group sessions is active learning, it is essential that each session be as student-centered as possible; this calls for a quite different behavior than the instructor is likely to be familiar with. Small group sessions are not meant to be lectures, although there will certainly be occasions when it is appropriate for the instructor to provide structured information. And instructor modelling of problem solving must be accompanied by opportunities for the students to practice the skills being modelled and opportunities to receive feedback about their performance. Furthermore, it is important that faculty be conscious of and able to support the group dynamics that are present so as to foster an atmosphere in the group for active learning. The behaviors expected of instructors in such sessions certainly need to be defined, and it may be necessary to assist faculty in learning the new skills that they are being asked to practice.[11,12]

How Will Student Problem Solving
Performance Be Assessed?

It has frequently been observed that examinations drive the curriculum to a much greater extent than any other form of motivation that instructors can bring to bear.[13] If all we do is announce that problem solving is important and then test only the ability to remember isolated facts, we can not expect our students to take seriously the claim that problem solving is important.

However, the manner in which we will assess student mastery of problem solving skills can be quite varied. Grading of laboratory reports, assigned problems, or projects is certainly one way to monitor student performance. Quizzes relating to laboratory or discussion-group sessions, and appropriate questions on examinations are other ways of accomplishing the same end.

As a practical matter, it is important to note that multiple choice questions can be used to test problem solving just as they can be used to test recall. Quantitative problems can be posed with multiple choice answers available (and student selection of appropriately generated incorrect choices can be diagnostic of student misconceptions). The ability to reason about the qualitative, causal relationships in a particular system can be tested by requiring the students to select sets of predictions about system responses.[14]

EXAMPLES OF SMALL GROUP SESSIONS

I will try to pull together these ideas by describing two examples of active, small group problem solving that have been implemented at Rush Medical College in our medical physiology course. These are not offered as ideals to be matched by your own sessions, but they do represent attempts to put into practice the ideas that have been described here.

Active Problem Solving in the Laboratory

Our course begins with a brief series of lectures on the function of the heart as a pump. This is accompanied by a laboratory exercise, the goal of which is to assist students to understand the sequence of events that make up the cardiac cycle. By "understand," we mean that students ought to be able to predict what set of events are occurring at the same time.

To assist students in developing a mental model of these phenomena, we have designed a laboratory experiment in which we record three important and easily accessible phenomena: the electrocardiogram (ECG), the heart sounds, and a carotid pulse (obtained noninvasively). Since the focus for this laboratory exercise is on integrating the occurrence of these three phenomena, not on the technical details of collecting the data, the protocol for this experiment calls for instructor demonstration (with student assistance) of each of these phenomena individually. As each recording is made the mechanisms at work are discussed *by the students* (to the fullest extent possible) and the students are asked to make predictions about the time of occurrence of other phenomena. Thus, the basic question that is put to each student is "what gives rise to this record and what other phenomena are occurring at the same time?" A dialogue results in which each of the students in the group is encouraged to think about the simultaneous events occurring during the cardiac cycle. And students can be asked to make predictions about when, relative to some particular event, some other thing occurs. Student comments about this laboratory have been uniformly positive, at least in part because it replaces rote memory with an active process that results in each individual students' generating the information to be mastered.

Active Problem Solving in the Discussion Section

In our course we place considerable importance on our students: (1) developing problem solving skills and (2) memorizing large numbers of "facts" (they clearly have to do this as well). Thus, we attempt to give the students opportunities to practice the problem solving that we deem to be important. For each of the major topic areas (more or less equivalent to organ systems) we schedule a "workshop," a small-group problem solving session (approximately 25 students) in which the faculty briefly demonstrate problem solving and then facilitate and critique the students' efforts at solving similar problems.

Each lecturer identifies the particular problems or phenomena that the students must understand, and problems are generated that will require the students to exercise the particular skills involved. For example, one problem presented data about the oxygen content at various locations in the circulation of a patient and required the students to calculate blood flow through the heart and then use the numbers obtained to determine the location of an abnormality in the circulation. Another problem required the students to reason about the consequences of an abnormally high concentration of a particular hormone. In each workshop the instructor first models the solution to the kind of problem being considered (and the focus with quantitative problems is always conceptual, not algebraic or arithmetic) and then the students divide up into 4–6 small groups to solve a similar problem, one they have not encountered before. When each group has cooperatively solved the problem the answers are put up on the board and these assembled results then serve to direct the discussion of the full workshop group about this problem. While the small groups are working at solving the assigned problem, the instructor is circulating among the groups trying to facilitate the problem solving process by answering questions or giving hints.

By the end of the workshop, each student has actively attacked a set of important problems in a defined area of physiology, has received assistance in solving such problems, and perhaps most importantly, has learned how much or how little he or she understands about the physiology under discussion.

THE IMPORTANCE OF "DETAILS" IN SHAPING STUDENT BEHAVIOR

The educational planning issues that I have discussed here are intended to bring about changes in student behavior; their goal is to assist students in making the transition from being passive to active learners, from memorizers to problem solvers. While there is a clear need to confront these global educational issues on the way to successful implementation of small group sessions, there are also a large number of implementation "details" that can dramatically impact the student behaviors we are seeking to shape.

While implementing the small group discussions described above we uncovered several such "details." Sessions are conducted in rooms with individual seating arranged in rows. When it was time to form the small problem solving groups, students were encouraged to form groups by arranging their chairs in circles. Often, however, what we saw were small clusters of students (2–3) interacting as a problem solving group only intermittently. When long tables were made available in the room, students were asked to sit around the table, and this change clearly resulted in greater group interaction. Similarly, group work was found to be facilitated when each group was given a single large piece of paper and instructed to develop their group answer on this page, rather than on their own sheets of notebook paper. Both of these "details" have had significant impact on facilitating the behaviors for which we have carried out so much course planning.

DISCUSSION AND CONCLUSIONS

Problem solving is a skill, and like any skill it must be practiced to be mastered. However, merely requiring students to solve problems is not in and of itself going to lead to the development of problem solving skills. Practice must be accompanied by corrective feedback, so that students have an opportunity to learn to reflect on their own performance; such metacognitive skills are an essential part of being an expert problem solver.[15]

It is possible for students to actively engage the material presented in lectures and textbooks. And it is possible for them to exercise spontaneously their problem solving skills as a component of their learning process. But, it is uncommon for either of these to occur to any appreciable extent in the usual lecture courses that we so often teach (however, for a discussion of promoting active learning and problem solving in a large group setting see the chapter by Modell and Carroll[16]). Active learning and problem solving is most often accomplished in a small group setting in which it is possible for an instructor to personally engage each student in the material and provide each student with feedback.

Small group sessions, whether they be laboratory experiments or discussion groups, are a potentially valuable opportunity for this kind of learning to occur. However, whether active learning *does* occur, and whether problem skills *do* get exercised is determined not by the size of the group but by what happens in the group. The key, then, lies in the implementation of small group sessions, and in this essay I have attempted to discuss some of the implementation issues that must be resolved if problem solving is to be learned in small groups.

ACKNOWLEDGMENTS

Dr. Allen Rovick and I have taught physiology together at Rush Medical College for almost 20 years, and for the past 10 years we have been collaborators on a number of research projects in which we have formally *studied* the teaching of physiology. Many of the ideas that I have developed here are the product of these years of lively discussions, debates, and arguments.

REFERENCES

1. MODELL, H. L. & J. A. MICHAEL. 1994. Ann. N.Y. Acad. Sci. This volume.
2. SHUELL, T. J. 1986. Cognitive conceptions of learning. Rev. Educ. Res. **56:** 411–436.
3. HEIMAN, M. 1987. Learning to learn: A behavioral approach to improving thinking. *In* Thinking: The Second International Conference. D. N. Perkins, J. Lochhead & J. Bishop, eds. : 431–452. Lawrence Erlbaum Associates. Hillsdale, NJ.
4. MAYER, R. E. 1983. Thinking, Problem Solving, Cognition. W. H. Freeman and Company. New York, NY.
5. FRASER, S. C., E. DIENER, A. BEARMAN & R. KELEM. 1977. Two, three or four heads are better than one: Modification of college performance by peer monitoring. J. Educ. Psychol. **69:** 101–108.
6. RANGACHARI, P. K. 1991. Design of a problem-based undergraduate course in pharmacology: Implications for the teaching of physiology. Am. J. Physiol. **260** (Advan. Physiol. Educ., 5) : S14–S21.
7. BARROWS, H. S. & R. M. TAMBLYN. 1980. Problem-based Learning: An Approach to Medical Education. Springer. New York, NY.
8. BARROWS, H. S. 1985. How to Design a Problem-based Curriculum for the Preclinical Years. Springer. New York, NY.
9. BOSSERT, S. T. 1988. Cooperative activities in the classroom. Rev. Res. Educ. **15:** 225–250.
10. GOODSELL, A., M. MAHER, V. TINTO, B. L. SMITH, & J. MACGREGOR. 1992. Collaborative Learning: A Sourcebook for Higher Education. National Center for Postsecondary Teaching, Learning and Assessment. University Park, PA.

11. Barrows, H. S. 1988. The Tutorial Process. Southern Illinois University School of Medicine. Springfield, IL.
12. Whitman, N. A. & T. L. Schwenk. 1983. A Handbook for Group Discussion Leaders: Alternatives to Lecturing Medical Students to Death. University of Utah School of Medicine. Salt Lake City, UT.
13. Neufeld, V. R. 1984. The design and use of assessment methods in problem-based learning. *In* Problem-based Learning. M. L. DeVolder, Eds. : 64–71. Van Gorcum. Assen, the Netherlands.
14. Rovick, A. A. & J. A. Michael. 1992. The prediction table: A tool for assessing students' knowledge. Am. J. Physiol. **263** (Advan. Physiol. Educ., **8**) : S33–S36.
15. Derry, S. J. & D. A. Murphy. 1986. Designing systems that train learning ability: From theory to practice. Rev. Educ. Res. **56:** 1–39.
16. Modell, H. L. & R. G. Carroll. 1994. Ann. N.Y. Acad. Sci. This volume.

Promoting Active Learning in Large Groups[a]

HAROLD I. MODELL[b] AND ROBERT G. CARROLL[c]

[b]*National Resource for Computers in Life Science Education*
Seattle, Washington 98115

[c]*Department of Physiology*
School of Medicine
East Carolina University
Greenville, North Carolina 27858

Promoting an active learning environment for any group of students may seem to be challenge, but doing so in a classroom with 75 or more students certainly appears, at first glance, to be a formidable task. It is, however, not as formidable as it may seem. Before dealing with the mechanics of turning the traditional "lecture hall" environment into one in which students become active learners, it is essential that we review some terms and define the role of faculty in an active learning environment.

ACTIVE LEARNING

We have defined an active learning environment as one in which students are personally engaged in the process of building and testing or applying their own mental models of the system under consideration.[1] This means that the student must be an active participant in the process. It is not enough to listen or watch as a body of information is presented for class consumption. The student must engage in a process that results in his or her internalizing the information and integrating that information into a personal conceptual framework that serves as the basis for his or her understanding of interactions within a system or between systems. In short, active learning requires the student to think about the information, not just record the information, and an active learning environment is one that encourages the student to engage in this process.

LARGE GROUPS

We generally think of a "large group" setting as one that shares the features of the lecture hall. Thus, although some student-to-student interaction may take place, the primary interaction is between the instructor and the group of students. In the context of this discussion, the feature that distinguishes a large group from a small group setting is that, in the large group setting, the instructor

[a]This work was funded in part by NIH Grant 1R43 DK44064-01.
[b]Address for correspondence: Harold I Modell, Ph.D., NRCLSE, P. O. Box 51187, Seattle, Washington 98115.

is not able to or chooses not to interact with each student on a one-to-one basis. Interaction with individual students may take place, but the intent of this interaction is to gain information about how the group is performing rather than to diagnose the progress of a specific individual. Although the term "large group" implies a significant class size (e.g., over 30 students), a "large group" setting may involve only a few students. The factor that distinguishes "large group" from "small group" settings is not the number of students, but rather the instructor's intent when interacting with the group.

ROLE OF THE FACULTY

Simply stated, the role of faculty in an active learning environment is to help the learner to learn. The first step, then, is for the faculty to recognize that the student is the focus of the learning process, and that in order to help the learner to learn, faculty must obtain feedback by interacting with the class on a regular basis. Furthermore, the interaction must be bidirectional. In the passive learning environment of the lecture hall, the lecturer may "interact" by asking rhetorical questions. In the active learning environment, the instructor challenges students to apply their current conceptual models to new situations (i.e., students must commit to an outcome based on their model), to generate new questions for themselves and seek answers to these questions, and to revise their mental models when necessary to accommodate new information. The faculty must change the classroom environment from one in which students view the instructor as a "purveyor of truth" to one in which they consider the instructor a resource in a joint learning effort.

ESTABLISHING THE "RULES OF THE GAME"

In general, students enter the classroom with a set of expectations, and their response to the educational environment in that classroom is related to those expectations. Currently, the expectations for a large group setting are often the result of, at minimum, several years of participation in an educational system based on the intake and recall of information. The experience common to most students is that they enroll in a course, the instructor tells them what they need to know to pass the exams, they are tested to see how well they have assimilated the prescribed information, and they receive a grade based on these factual recall examinations. The pattern is remarkably similar across disciplines. The lecturer dispenses knowledge, and the students are the passive recipients of that knowledge. Time is at a premium, so any classroom activity that appears to compromise the efficiency of the information transfer is viewed by students as nonproductive. It is, after all, this information transfer that forms the basis for exams, and hence for the reward system in which the student operates.

If we expect students to engage in active learning, a process in which they are required to think about rather than merely record the content, it is critical that their expectations be consistent with the educational goals of this learning environment. If student expectations are not consistent with this approach, the students will not only be uncooperative, they may actively rebel. Thus, it is imperative that the instructor explicitly define the "rules of the game" at the first meeting of the class. In doing so, the message must be clear that the course grade depends on the ability to integrate facts and think about the systems covered in the course rather than on the ability to merely recall facts. It is also important at this time to emphasize that the instructor is a facilitator whose goal it is to help the learner to learn; that students and instructor will be engaged in a cooperative relationship rather than an adversarial one.

In our experience, once students are made aware of the rules of the game, they are not only willing to modify their expectations for the class, but they enter into the active learning environment contract with a significant degree of enthusiasm. Having made this commitment, though, they fully expect the instructor to also abide by the rules of the game. Thus, care must be taken to ensure that the examinations are not merely exercises in recalling factual details, but are, in fact, designed to assess students' abilities to think about the system.

HELPING THE LEARNER TO LEARN

If our primary educational goal is to help the learner to learn, we must consider what types of activities might help us achieve that goal. In a very broad sense, we can divide the learning process into three stages; acquiring information, integrating that information into a personal conceptual framework or model, and testing the validity of that model.

We acquire information most efficiently when we perceive a need for that information. That is, we seek answers to questions, and we are most motivated to seek those answers when we, ourselves, ask the questions. In the traditional (passive) lecture environment, information is disseminated with little regard to whether the student is seeking specific information. In the active learning environment, the instructor also disseminates information, but he or she first helps the student develop a personal need to seek that information. Thus, one category of activities consists of exercises designed to focus students' attention on the topic at hand and help them ask questions for which they will subsequently seek answers.

The cognitive processes through which we integrate information into a personal conceptual framework have not been fully explored. Nevertheless, we can draw on our own experience to identify some factors that play a role in this process. For example, we are better able to "understand" concepts that relate to our existing knowledge and our current mental models. Furthermore, as we acquire new sensory information that relates to specific concepts, we are better able to extend our current mental models or develop new, more robust models. This leads to a second category of activities designed to help students relate concepts to their existing knowledge and to provide them with the opportunity to experience the manifestations of a concept more intimately.

A third category of activities are those designed to help students test their own mental models. Testing the validity of a model necessitates making a prediction (i.e., a commitment to an outcome) and determining the accuracy of that prediction. When designing activities in this category, it is important to recognize that some students may not have developed their mental model to the point where a specific prediction can be made. In this case, "I don't know" is a valid response and one that should be included as an option.

SPECIFIC EXAMPLES

After establishing broad categories of classroom activities based on educational goals, it is useful to consider examples of specific activities to help visualize how active learning can be facilitated in a large group setting. Some activities require advanced planning, but others are spontaneous and are the result of the realization that the instructor's job is to help the learner to learn. We have chosen examples from the realm of cardiopulmonary physiology, although, as it will become clear, the underlying techniques can be applied to any content area.

EDUCATIONAL OBJECTIVE: TO FOCUS STUDENT ATTENTION

The following two examples illustrate different approaches to motivating students to seek additional information about the topic at hand. In the first example, the "lecture" topics are the mechanical properties of the respiratory system and neuroregulation of ventilation. In this example, the instructor initially provides the questions, but through an active effort by the students, the class members relate the questions to their own bodies, thereby personalizing the quest.

The students are told to close their eyes and concentrate on their breathing. After a short time (30–45 seconds, enough time for students to focus on several breaths), the instructor asks, "What happened?" and solicits responses from the class. The questioning then gets more detailed. "Did you rest at the end of inspiration or at the end of expiration?" In this case, individual verbal responses can be solicited or a show of hands can be requested. If some students answer that they rested at the end of inspiration, they are directed to close their eyes again and concentrate again on their breathing. In this way, they are testing their own hypothesis (rest at the end of inspiration) and discovering that the data do not support their hypothesis. The questioning continues with an occasional repeat of the breathing exercise. What determines the lung volume at the end of expiration? That is, why did the system stop where it stopped? What caused air to flow into your lungs when you inspired? What forces had to be overcome before this flow would take place? Having established some key questions, the class session can continue with the aim of exploring the mechanical properties of the respiratory system so that these questions can be answered. At any relevant point in the discussion, the breathing exercise can be repeated to help the students relate what is being discussed to their own personal frame of reference.

The second example is designed to help students apply their current mental models to a new situation as well as generate questions for which answers will be sought during the class session. The topic this time is the cardiac cycle. Each student is given a piece of paper containing axes representing pressure versus time and volume versus time (FIG. 1). An electrocardiogram is shown on the same time axis. The students are familiar with ideas of a pump and valves directing flow. The task, then, is to describe how pressure in the left atrium, left ventricle, and aorta, and the volume of the left ventricle vary with time during the one cardiac cycle represented by the electrocardiogram trace. Students are told to work in groups of no less than three and no more than five students drawn from those people sitting around them. A group of this size is small enough to allow all group members to participate in the discussion. The class is given 5–10 minutes to work on the problem. After the allotted time, the class session continues with a discussion of the cardiac cycle.

Several outcomes result from this exercise. First, student attention is focused on the topic of the day. Hence, when the class discussion begins, students have already "shifted gears" from the world outside the classroom to that inside the classroom. Second, they have begun to relate "new" information (the cardiac style) to their existing models of pumps and valves. They have articulated this extension of their current mental models to their peers and, in some cases, have had to defend their position. In some cases, this discussion has raised questions for students who will look to the remainder of the class session for answers.

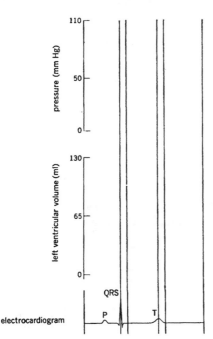

FIGURE 1. Example of a problem on a handout given to students prior to beginning the discussion of the cardiac cycle. Before the discussion, students are asked to describe how pressure in the left atrium, left ventricle, and aorta, and the volume of the left ventricle vary with time during one cardiac cycle (see text).

Finally, they have generated a prediction, based on their models and discussions with peers, of the information that will be presented in the overall class discussion. It is important to emphasize that the plots generated by the students are not in any way intended to be an assessment tool for grading purposes. The exercise is designed to allow students to draw on their own knowledge to generate hypotheses that they can test during the remainder of the class discussion.

EDUCATIONAL OBJECTIVE: TO HELP STUDENTS RELATE CONCEPTS TO THEIR EXISTING KNOWLEDGE

Before one can help students relate concepts to their existing frames of reference, it is necessary either to learn how they view the "world" or to have each student relate his or her personal view to a common frame of reference. The lecturer in a passive learning environment tries to do this by defining the frame of reference. However, little time is afforded the students to make the necessary connection with their own views. The alternative for an active learning environment is to ask the students about their conceptual views. This is easily done by showing a schematic drawing, a data plot, a photo, or some other visual aid related to the concept under discussion and asking class members what they see. (In other cases, the choice might be an audible signal with the question, "What do you hear?") An example of a schematic diagram used in this way is shown in FIGURE. 2. The graphic deals with the way in which oxygen and carbon dioxide are carried in blood. The goal of the exercise is to have students realize four key points: that the two processes are similar in principle; that the partial pressure of gas in blood is related to the dissolved gas; that there is a relationship between the partial pressure and the "bound" gas; and that the two processes

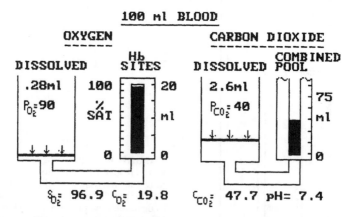

FIGURE 2. Graphic illustration showing how oxygen and carbon dioxide are carried in blood. The graphic is shown to the class, and the instructor asks the class members to describe what they see (see text).

differ in that the amount of oxygen carried in a "bound" form reaches a limit, while the amount of carbon dioxide carried in forms other than dissolved gas does not reach a limit in the physiological range.

The exercise, then, is to show the class the graphic and direct the class to "tell me what you see." Volunteers can be solicited, specific students can be called on, or the instructor can attempt to identify answers from the general level of mumbling. Each point can then be discussed and elaborated on as the class focuses on one part of the graphic or another. The key element is that the class members (i.e., the learners) are directing the focus of the discussion.

Asking "what do you see?" is very different from asking "what will happen if . . . ?" The former question is nonjudgmental, and, from the student's standpoint, there is no right or wrong answer. It is a nonthreatening request for which all students have an answer. All sighted students see something, and individual students are more willing to share their observations with the class than they are to voice answers to questions that have what they perceive as a "correct" answer.

The result of the exercise is that the discussion revolves around the perspective of the class members rather than the perspective of the instructor.

EDUCATIONAL OBJECTIVE:
TO ENABLE STUDENTS TO EXPERIENCE THE
MANIFESTATIONS OF A CONCEPT MORE INTIMATELY

Example 1:

This exercise is used in conjunction with a discussion of elastic structures (e.g., lungs, the total respiratory system, heart, blood vessels). The goals of such a discussion are to have students understand the following points:

1. Elastic structures have a resting or unstressed volume at which the transmural pressure is zero.

2. A transmural pressure must be imposed on the structure to oppose its elastic recoil and displace it from its unstressed volume (positive to increase volume, negative to decrease volume).

3. Compliance is a measure of the pressure change needed to effect a volume change.

In a passive learning environment, the instructor may choose to demonstrate these points by inflating or deflating a common model of an elastic structure (e.g., a balloon). When watching the demonstration, the students receive only visual and auditory information. One approach to the discussion in an active learning environment is to provide each student with a balloon and have each student perform some experiments through which they can explore the concepts of recoil and compliance. In this case, the student receives the same type of visual and auditory information as in the lecture, but he or she also receives other sensory information with which to relate the concepts. The student must generate a pressure to blow up the balloon, and, in doing so, he feels the force necessary to overcome the elastic recoil of the balloon. After the balloon is inflated, and the student is holding the balloon's neck so that it will not deflate, she feels the pressure generated by the balloon's recoil. If the student continues to inflate the balloon, she senses that it is harder to inflate (i.e., its compliance decreases) as the balloon's elastic limit is approached.

The exercise personalizes the experience. The student is no longer relating the vocabulary and the concepts discussed to what the instructor has done, but rather what he or she has done.

Example 2:

The following activity was first used in the classroom in response to a student-generated question about the relationship between pacemaker cells in the heart. The goal of the exercise was to help the class relate to the pacemaker cells governing cardiac muscle contraction by making them an integral part of an analogy of the system.

Three students were chosen from the group. Student A was told to clap his hands in a regular rhythm. Student B was told that she, also, had a natural tendency to clap in a regular rhythm, but her "natural rhythm" was slower than student A's. Furthermore, whenever she heard student A clap, she was obliged to clap. Student C was directed to clap whenever she heard student B clap. The exercise was begun, and it was clear that the remainder of the group mentally took on the role of each of the "cardiac cell" students as it was his or her time to clap. Student A then stopped clapping, and the pacemaker function for this model system moved from student A to student B. The analogy helped the students understand why the pacemaker cell with the highest depolarization frequency governs heart rate.

Both of these examples put the student at the center of the learning process. In each case, the goal is to help the student personally experience some aspect of the concept or mechanism under discussion.

EDUCATIONAL OBJECTIVE:
TO HELP STUDENTS TEST OR APPLY THEIR MENTAL
MODELS OF THE SYSTEM UNDER CONSIDERATION

As with the other categories discussed, there is a spectrum of techniques that can be used to help students test their mental models. They all, however, are based on the same assumption. One of the many "Murphy's Law" publications (Price/Stern/Sloan Publishers, Inc., Los Angeles) in the past decade included Natalie's Law of Algebra that states that "You never catch on until after the test." If, as experience suggests, there is some truth to Natalie's Law of Algebra, it is interesting to speculate about what it is about the test, per se, that makes the difference in the learning process. The test requires that the student use his or her mental model of the system in a problem solving process to produce a result. The student has made a commitment to his or her mental model, and, after making the commitment, he or she gathers data (i.e., the "correct" answer) with which to reevaluate and modify the model if necessary. The assumption, then, that underlies the following examples is that the critical element in the process is making a commitment based on the mental model, and the goal of each activity is to have students commit to a prediction.

In the course of an ongoing discussion, this can be done by asking for a show of hands. "Will this variable increase, decrease, or stay the same?" It is often helpful to ask people making the wrong prediction for the basis of their prediction. The purpose is, again, to help the learner to learn. If a significant portion of the class makes the wrong prediction, identifying the flaw in the rationale before the "correct" answer is made known will help students reexamine and modify their mental models without attaching a value judgment to the original prediction. It is helpful to remember that, in this type of exercise, "I don't know" is often valid response, and, for the instructor, becomes a powerful assessment tool to identify where students are having trouble understanding the concepts being discussed. In fact, other responses should also be considered as valid in certain circumstances to help the instructor better understand various factors that may impact on the learner's ability to concentrate at the moment. For example, "It's the end of the day, we've been sitting in class for four hours, and we're just too tired to think" indicates that an analogy requiring physical participation by the students may be more helpful than a discussion focused on a set of slides.

A second activity that forces students to make a commitment is to present a problem that extends the current discussion, have the students work on it for a few minutes in groups of 3–5 students, and subsequently solicit responses from representatives of the groups to initiate a discussion of the problem. For example, after discussing the cardiac cycle, present the class with a description of a heart valve disorder. The task for the small groups is to predict the immediate and long term effects of the disorder on the pressure and volume curves that formed the basis of the cardiac cycle discussion.

A computer simulation used in conjunction with a suitable projection device can serve as an excellent vehicle to help students test their mental models of a system. The following example illustrates one application of such a simulation. An output screen from a simulation dealing with alveolar gas exchange is shown in FIGURE. 3. In this simulation, the user provides values for tidal volume, frequency, dead space volume, and oxygen consumption. The computer returns the minute ventilation ($\dot{V}_E$), alveolar ventilation ($\dot{V}_A$), alveolar gas tensions, and mixed expired gas tensions.

Having discussed the simplifying assumptions that underlie the model, the instructor, after consultation with the class, enters the normal control values and obtains the screen shown in FIGURE. 3. After discussing these data (Do these results make sense?), the instructor poses a question, "How can we increase our ventilation?" The class will suggest that we can either breathe deeper (increase tidal volume), or we can breathe faster (increase frequency). To direct the class toward an experiment, the instructor then asks, "Does it make a difference, in terms of gas exchange, whether tidal volume or frequency is increased?" The class then decides whether frequency or tidal volume should be increased and by how much. Before entering the new values, however, the instructor asks the students to record their predictions of what will happen to the various output variables as a result of the change in frequency or tidal volume. Alternatively,

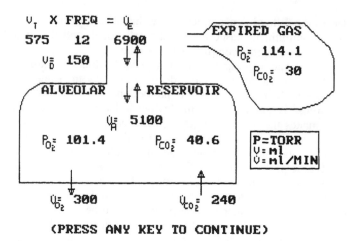

FIGURE 3. Representation of output screen from a computer simulation dealing with alveolar gas exchange. The user supplies values for tidal volume (V_T), frequency (FREQ), anatomical dead space volume (V_D), and oxygen consumption ($\dot{V}_{O_2}$). The gas exchange ratio is assumed to be 0.8, so carbon dioxide production is fixed as soon as a value for oxygen consumption is supplied. The program calculates minute ventilation ($\dot{V}_E$), alveolar ventilation ($\dot{V}_A$), and the alveolar and mixed expired partial pressures of oxygen and carbon dioxide.

the instructor may ask for a show of hands of those people who think alveolar oxygen tension, for example, will increase, decrease, or stay constant. Again, the purpose of the exercise at this point is to have the students commit to a prediction. It is irrelevant at this stage if their predictions are correct. The experiment is run, the computer displays the data, and the students determine whether their predictions were right or wrong. At this point, however, the instructor is obligated to lead a discussion explaining why the input values resulted in this set of output values.

These are but three representative activities illustrating how students can be involved in an active learning exercise designed to test or apply their mental models. A large number of possibilities exist for other activities. Some require no technology, some require "technology" that can be found in the home or local grocery store, and others require computer or multi-media technology of various degrees of sophistication. Again, if the attitude of the instructor is to help the learner to learn, technology is not essential to fostering an active learning environment in the classroom.

APPARENT LIMITATION OF THE
ACTIVE LEARNING ENVIRONMENT

When first introduced to the idea of replacing the traditional lecture presentation with an active learning environment, colleagues invariably raise the criticism that, in the active learning approach, one cannot cover all of the material that must be covered in a modern life science course. In fact, it is true that one cannot cover as much material with this approach. However, the criticism is based on the premise that the faculty's primary responsibility is to disseminate all of the information for which the student is responsible; in essence, to tell the students all that they need to know. If, indeed, this is the role of the faculty, then the active learning approach should not be attempted. After all, the passive learning environment of the traditional lecture hall may represent the most efficient classroom environment in which to present a body of information.

The criticism is not valid, however, if the role of the faculty is to help students learn how to think about a body of information and how to use that body of information to seek new answers to new challenges (i.e., to learn the process of science). The issue is not how much material can be covered in the course, but, rather, how class time is to be used. If the intended role of the active learning environment is made clear to the students when the "rules of the game" are defined, the same amount of factual material can be covered in the course. The difference is that the textbook or similar resources become the primary source of the factual knowledge base rather than the lecture hall.

Another issue often raised by colleagues is the degree of participation by members of the class. There always seem to be a few students who, for one reason or another, refuse to commit themselves publicly by raising their hands or contributing to a discussion. The challenge appears to be how to get these students involved in the process. However, the critical element of the process is to have students make a commitment to themselves, that is, predict an outcome based on their understanding of the system. It is not essential that all students share their predictions with classmates or the instructor. We have, on occasion, asked "nonparticipating" students privately what they were thinking when the other class members responded to a request for a show of hands or when other students were responding to the "tell me what you see" request. They indicated that they, too, were involved in the same thought process as their peers. They were just not comfortable sharing that information. Hence, the goal of involving these students in an active learning exercise was also achieved.

CONCLUSION

The key factor in transforming the passive lecture hall environment into a large group active learning environment is the instructor's view of his or her reason for being in the classroom. Once one adopts the attitude that the role of the "teacher" is to help the learner to learn rather than to impart knowledge to the student, the various types of activities described above become a natural part of faculty-student interactions.

If we, as scientists, expect our students to (1) recognize that science is not a collection of facts described by a specialized vocabulary but is a process through which we come to know about the world in which we live, and (2) learn to become adept at engaging in that process, we must provide them with an opportunity to practice the skills necessary to engage in that process. As with any skill, one must practice thinking to become proficient in thinking skills. Promoting an active learning environment in the classroom provides students with a model (i.e., the instructor) of how to engage in this activity and provides an opportunity for the students to practice using the process. If this is not justification enough to adopt the view of the teacher as a facilitator, perhaps the observation voiced by a colleague after participating in a demonstration of passive versus active learning will help. The colleague noted that the active learning environment makes teaching fun again.

REFERENCE

1. MODELL, H. I. & J. A. MICHAEL. 1993. Promoting active learning in the life science classroom: Defining the issues. Ann. N.Y. Acad. Sci. This volume.

Classroom Assessment:
Assessing to Improve Higher Learning in the Life Sciences

THOMAS ANTHONY ANGELO

Academic Development Center
The Connors Learning Center
Boston College
Chestnut Hill, Massachusetts 02167-3810

OVERVIEW

This paper has six main objectives. First, it argues that current efforts to promote active student involvement are necessary but not sufficient to guarantee better learning in the life sciences. Second, it suggests that faculty can make their instructional improvement efforts more effective by practicing Classroom Assessment. *Classroom Assessment* can be described as a simple method for getting feedback, early and often, on what, how well, and how students are learning, and using that feedback to improve learning. Third, the paper describes five critical dimensions of higher learning in the life sciences which can be assessed and enhanced with simple Classroom Assessment techniques. These five dimensions are (1) learning the facts, principles, and concepts of the discipline; (2) developing the relevant skills; (3) learning to transfer and apply knowledge and skills to new situations; (4) developing self-awareness of opinions, attitudes and values related to the discipline; and, (5) developing metacognitive awareness and skills.

Fourth, the paper offers examples of how faculty in several different life sciences and related fields—including anatomy and physiology, biology, chemistry, environmental studies, mathematics, physics, physiology, and zoology—use Classroom Assessment to better understand and improve their students' learning across these dimensions. Fifth, it summarizes faculty views of the "costs and benefits" of using Classroom Assessment. And, lastly, it suggests a few practical guidelines, based on several years of field experience, that can help life sciences faculty use Classroom Assessment effectively.

THE CRISIS: QUANTITY OF STUDENTS,
QUALITY OF LEARNING

The current crisis in science education in the United States is well-documented and much lamented. In higher education, it is a crisis both of quantity and of quality. The science education "pipeline" is extraordinarily leaky, and particularly so for women and other traditionally underrepresented groups. Stated simply, far too few U.S. college students major in the sciences in the first

61

place, and far too many of those students drop out of the sciences before graduating. At the same time, far too many non-science majors learn too little of lasting consequence in their required science courses, and far too few of them go on to take any further courses in the sciences.

The reasons for this crisis in American science education have been widely discussed and debated, and many possible solutions have been suggested.[1,2] While it is true that some of the reasons behind this crisis are not under the control of faculty, individual teachers can contribute to its solution. Teachers certainly influence how much and how well students learn in individual classes. Further, evidence from recent research[3,4] indicates that the quality of teaching and advising that students receive strongly influences their decisions to stay in or drop out of science, math, and engineering programs. This suggests that individual science teachers can play important roles in increasing both the quantity of science graduates and the quality of their learning by improving the quality of science instruction in their own classrooms.

ONE POTENTIAL SOLUTION: PROMOTING ACTIVE INVOLVEMENT IN LEARNING

Educational research and practice have long demonstrated that higher levels of active student involvement in learning are usually correlated with higher academic achievement.[5] In response, many science departments have revised their curricula, and individual professors have reworked their syllabi, to include more opportunities for active learning. But as Joan Stark, Professor of Higher Education at the University of Michigan, has pointed out, there are really three co-existing, and sometimes very different curricula: the curriculum described in our course catalogs and syllabi, the curriculum faculty actually teach, and the curriculum students actually learn. As a consequence, improving the "written" and the "taught" curricula will have little impact on student achievement in life sciences unless the "learned" curriculum is also improved.

Whether or not they are aware of the relevant educational research, most life sciences faculty realize that actively involving students is critical to improving learning. In hopes of promoting more active engagement in the "taught" curriculum, many college science teachers have revised their syllabi and teaching plans to include activities such as discussions, debates, questioning, in-class writing, group problem solving exercises, role-playing, simulations and games, and peer teaching. While such changes are likely to be productive, it is nevertheless true that more activity, in and of itself, is no guarantee of more and better learning. As George Stoddard put it: "We learn to do neither by thinking nor by doing; we learn to do by thinking about what we are doing." For active learning to be most effective, students need timely, regular, comprehensible feedback from teachers. They need this feedback to effectively direct, monitor, and make the most of their active involvement in academic work. At the same time, students need help learning to self-assess in order to become successful, independent learners.

Faculty need feedback on their students' learning, as well. Unless teachers gauge the impact of curriculum and instruction on learning before making revisions, they risk shooting in the dark. And unless faculty then assess the impact of changes made in syllabi and of teaching behaviors on student learning, they will have no way of knowing if, when, how much, and what kind of changes our innovations have provoked—or what next steps are called for. In other words, without assessment, faculty run the risk of changing for change's sake, without clear justification or direction, and the risk of making things worse, not better. To guide their ongoing attempts to close the gaps between the "written," "taught," and "learned" curricula, faculty need simple, effective ways to assess learning in the classroom.

CLASSROOM ASSESSMENT: DEFINITION AND PURPOSE

Classroom Assessment is a simple, straightforward method faculty can use to collect feedback, early and often, on how well their students are actually learning what is being taught. To improve learning, teachers use feedback and insights gleaned through Classroom Assessments to make informed adjustments in their teaching. Just as important, faculty share that feedback with students, helping them to improve their study skills and learning strategies and, ultimately, to become more effective, responsible, and independent learners.

Since the word "assessment" is subject to a wide range of interpretations, it is important to clarify its meaning here in relation to my use of the term "Classroom Assessment." K. Patricia Cross draws the following useful distinctions:

> Most people think of assessment as a *large-scale* testing program, conducted at *institutional or state* levels, usually by *measurement experts*, to determine what students *have* learned in *college*. Classroom Assessment questions almost every working word of that definition. A definition of Classroom Assessment looks more like this: Classroom Assessment consists of *small-scale* assessments conducted *continuously* in college classrooms by discipline-based *teachers* to determine what students *are* learning in *that class*.[6] (italics in original)

The purpose of many large-scale assessment programs is primarily to provide accountability to administrators, elected officials, or the public, and only secondarily and indirectly to improve teaching and learning. Assessments which occur at the end of the process and that are aimed primarily at providing accountability are usually referred to as "summative" assessments. That is, they "sum up" what has been learned or accomplished. This summative focus helps to explain why many faculty perceive assessment efforts to be, at worst, a threat to their academic freedom, or, at best, another time-wasting example of "adminis-trivia."

The primary purpose of Classroom Assessment, by contrast, is to improve learning *in progress* by providing teachers with the kind of feedback they need to guide their day-to-day instructional decisions—and by providing students with information that can help them learn more effectively. Assessment that takes place during the teaching-learning process, and that is aimed primarily at improvement, is known as "formative" assessment. This simply means that it gives form and purpose to the process in progress. Classroom Assessment, then, is a type of formative assessment.

The simple "tools" teachers use to collect student feedback are known as Classroom Assessment Techniques, or CATs. At first, faculty are prone to confuse Classroom Assessment Techniques (CATs) with the tests and quizzes they commonly use to evaluate student learning—or with familiar teaching techniques. Unlike tests or quizzes, however, CATs are ungraded and usually anonymous. And the unit of analysis is different. The purpose of Classroom Assessments is to assess the whole class's learning in order to adjust instruction; not to evaluate the achievement of individual students in order to assign grades. Put another way, if the primary purpose of tests and quizzes is to rate and rank learn*ers,* the aim of Classroom Assessment is to understand and improve learn*ing.*

Classroom Assessment Techniques are not tests, but neither are they simply teaching techniques. CATs are meant to be used *between* teaching and testing, to find out how well students are doing in time to help them improve. Explicitly or implicitly, all faculty already use teaching techniques to achieve their instructional goals. Several thousand faculty now use Classroom Assessment Techniques to find out how well they are achieving those goals while there is still time for them and students to make adjustments. By way of analogy, CATs are to teaching techniques as diagnostic fitness tests are to exercise routines.

A third possible confusion concerns the relationship between Classroom Assessment and teacher evaluation. On most campuses, teacher evaluation is a form of summative evaluation. Typically, college teachers and their teaching are evaluated by students at the end of the term and that information is used—if it is used at all—in making decisions about retention, tenure, and promotion. Teacher evaluation can be a useful source of reliable and valid information on how well faculty are teaching. And, in fairness, some departments and colleges do use teacher evaluation to help faculty improve their teaching. In most cases, however, teacher evaluation is a type of *post hoc,* summative evaluation that does little or nothing to improve the quality of teaching or learning.

While teacher evaluation—whether summative or formative—is focused on teachers and teaching, Classroom Assessment focuses on learners and learning. Moreover, Classroom Assessment, in contrast to teacher evaluation, is teacher-directed. That means that the individual faculty who use Classroom Assessment have control over every step of the process. In Classroom Assessments, unlike student evaluations, each teacher decides what questions to ask and what kind of information to collect, how to collect that feedback and how to analyze it, with whom to share the results of their Classroom Assessments, and what changes, if any, to make in response to those results. So, although Classroom

Assessment can provide faculty with information on the effectiveness of their teaching, it is primarily for gathering information to help teachers and students understand the learning process and improve its quality.

FIVE DIMENSIONS OF HIGHER LEARNING

Before faculty can meaningfully assess student learning, they need to identify the specific kinds of learning they are trying to promote. In my own teaching, I've found it useful to categorize learning into five distinct, though interrelated, dimensions.

Dimension One: Declarative Learning (Learning What)

Simply put, declarative learning in higher education is learning the terms, facts, principles, and concepts of a given field—learning the "what" of the discipline. Since we can usually find out how well students have learned relevant facts, principles, and concepts by asking them to declare in speech or writing what they know, psychologists call this declarative learning. When we teach students the definitions of alveolar ventilation, the elements of the periodic table, the Linnaean system of classification, Kepler's laws of planetary motion, or the concept of evolution, we are promoting declarative learning.

College science teachers are particularly interested in declarative learning. In a survey of more than 2,800 two- and four-year college faculty, 55% of the science teachers responding indicated that "teaching facts and principles" was their primary role. By contrast, about 28% of the science faculty chose "developing higher-order thinking skills" as their primary role.[7] Many science faculty feel frustrated in their efforts to "cover" exponentially expanding course content, and most students in the life sciences are acutely aware of the massive amount of information they are expected to learn.

Dimension Two: Procedural Learning (Learning How)

While knowledge of facts and principles is necessary to higher learning, it is hardly sufficient. Students must also develop skills. There are some skills that all college students are expected to master (such as thinking, speaking, and writing clearly) and many courses are designed to promote this general level of procedural learning. Thus, each academic discipline is defined both by the particular body of (declarative) knowledge that its aspiring members are expected to learn, and also by a collection of discipline-specific skills they must master. The mix of general and specific skills taught in colleges and universities make up the procedural dimension of learning.

In life sciences, there are many very discipline-specific intellectual and laboratory skills to be mastered, along with more general scientific problem solving skills. For example, students in introductory chemistry courses must not only learn *what* Avogadro's number is, but also *how* to calculate it. In lower-division botany courses, students learn how to classify unfamiliar plants.

Dimension Three: Conditional Learning (Learning When and Where)

Although the third dimension is less often explicitly taught than the first two, it is nonetheless a critical element in a meaningful higher education. Its name refers to the learner's ability to evaluate the conditions under which the application of declarative and procedural knowledge is likely to be most successful. In plain language, conditional learning is learning to exercise good judgment in a particular field. It is knowing when and where to use what you know to greatest advantage.

Two quick examples may help to illustrate the conditional dimension. A physics major may demonstrate mastery in classical mechanics but be unable to see its applications to the biomechanics of human locomotion. A graduate student in statistics may learn how to perform the various tests for statistical significance, but if that same student cannot decide which test to apply in the context of a given "real world" research problem, those skills and that knowledge will be of little use.

To the extent that we teach conditional learning, it is often done through the use of examples and modeling. The case study method and clinical instruction, two teaching methods widely used in professional education, often focus directly on developing applications, transfer, and judgment—as does one-on-one coaching. In the life sciences, students are often expected to learn applications through course-related laboratory experiments and later work as research assistants. Conditional learning is especially important for those students studying life sciences as preparation for careers in medicine and health-related fields who must become adept at transferring and applying prior knowledge to new situations.

Dimension Four: Reflective Learning (Learning Why)

As important as the first three dimensions of higher learning are, even their mastery is not enough to qualify a student as a liberally educated person within our tradition. To constitute more than expensive job training, higher education must also help students develop the habits of mind and heart required for the full exercise of citizenship and the responsible pursuit of individual happiness. To become independent, life-long learners, students need to gain insights into their own interests, motivations, attitudes, and values. In short, students need to learn to be self-reflective, to understand why they believe, think, and act as they do—and to value self-reflection.

In many U.S. universities, this dimension of learning is dealt with—if at all—in the general education curriculum, or in career counseling and other personal development courses. But in each academic field, there are particular questions of personal values, beliefs, and attitudes that students must confront in order to understand and participate fully in the "culture" of that discipline. For example, in all of the life sciences, advances in genetic research and engineering are raising complex ethical and moral questions of great importance. In the health-related fields, these questions arise daily in relation to the use or withholding of expensive and often intrusive means to treat diseases and extend life.

Dimension Five: Metacognitive Learning (Learning about Learning)

To become more effective learners and, eventually, to achieve success in their careers, students need to develop their metacognitive abilities as well. That is, they need to become better able to reflect on, understand, and direct and control their own thinking processes. Metacognition requires making implicit cognitive processes explicit and manipulable. In the life sciences, for example, students need to become fluent problem solvers, but they also need to develop the ability to "look over their own shoulders" as they solve problems, to evaluate their problem solving routines, and to make adjustments as needed.

EXAMPLES OF CLASSROOM ASSESSMENT IN FIVE DIMENSIONS

The brief examples that follow are meant to suggest simple means for assessing student learning—in life sciences and related disciplines—in each of the five dimensions outlined above. While each example focuses on assessing a single dimension, this approach is merely a useful simplification. In reality, of course, effective learning is always multidimensional, and the learning of content, skills, applications, and self-awareness are interrelated and mutually reinforcing. Consequently, assessing and promoting learning in one dimension often helps improve learning overall. The following examples[7,8] draw heavily on the experiences of many colleagues whose contributions I wish to acknowledge. Though details have been changed and situations greatly simplified, their dedication, experience, and creativity inform every example.

ASSESSING DECLARATIVE LEARNING

In Chemistry

On the first day of class, a chemistry professor asked students in his large introductory course to give chemistry-related examples of three key terms—data, law, and theory—that students would encounter frequently in subsequent lectures and readings. In other words, he wanted to assess whether his students could provide plausible, discipline-specific examples of a data statement, a scientific law, and a theoretical statement. He used a CAT we call the Misconception/Preconception Check,[7] a simple way to get feedback on students' prior knowledge.

The chemistry instructor explained that he was not too concerned about the correctness of the examples, only their appropriateness. He assured students it was not a test, and reminded them *not* to put their names on the papers. After giving students ten minutes in class to write their examples, he collected them.

In reading through their responses later that day, the instructor found that over 70% of the class could produce an acceptable data statement, but less than 20% could provide a statement of theory or a law. Faced with this evidence, he realized he could no longer assume, as he had for more than twenty years, that students arrived with useful conceptions of basic, key terms. In the subsequent class session, he followed up by using students' responses, correct and incorrect, to explicitly teach the concepts of law and theory as applied to chemistry.

In Anatomy and Physiology

In a course designed for future nurses, a biology professor stressed the importance of understanding the connections between structures, functions, and processes. To assess how well his first-year students were making these connections in relation to the digestive system, he created a Memory Matrix.[7] The matrix consisted of three columns—labeled "structure," "function," and "enzymes"—intersected by eight rows, each representing one of the digestive organs. The organs he included were the mouth, esophagus, stomach, small and large intestines, pancreas, liver, and gall bladder. The empty matrix was a rectangle containing twenty-four boxes in which students could write answers.

A firm believer in cooperative learning, the instructor divided the class of forty into eight groups of five, then handed each group one oversized copy of the empty Memory Matrix. He gave the groups fifteen minutes to fill in the critical, missing information. A flurry of activity took place as groups scrambled to complete their matrices. When time was up, he collected the eight large sheets. During the next twenty minutes, as the students watched a videotape on enzyme functioning, the instructor quickly scanned the assessments, looking for missing, misplaced and incorrect information. He made a rough tally of correct responses on his own master sheet, then noted the patterns. He used this information to selectively review the digestive system during the last third of the class session.

ASSESSING PROCEDURAL LEARNING

In Zoology

After two weeks of work on mammals, and two weeks before the first test, this zoology professor decided to assess his students' skill at categorizing mammals visually. He did the assessment in two stages. For both, he provided students with mimeographed Categorizing Grids,[7] projected numbered slides, and directed students to write the slide numbers in the correct boxes on the grids.

On Monday, for the first stage, he gave students a Categorizing Grid divided into three boxes for the three mammalian subclasses: Prototheria, Metatheria, and Eutheria. He then projected thirty slides in rapid succession, with examples more or less evenly divided among subclasses. Skimming the grids, he was pleased but not surprised to find that the class did quite well, with only a few minor confusions. At the end of the next class meeting, on Wednesday, he handed out a new, more complex grid, and asked students to categorize thirty-five slides of the subclass Eutheria into seven of its major orders. The results on the second stage were very uneven, with about half the class doing very well; the other half, rather poorly. On Friday, he quickly went over the results of both assessments and suggested strategies for reviewing the material. He reminded students that the first test would require exactly this type of categorizing and suggested that they study together, sharing their strategies for mastering this skill.

In Mathematics

To better understand how well his students' problem solving skills were developing, a veteran calculus teacher adapted the Documented Problem Solution technique[7] in a clever way that allowed him to get more feedback on their learning of these critical skills without increasing his overall workload. Specifically, the instructor substituted the CAT for part of an existing homework assignment. Instead of assigning and grading five homework problems each class session, as he had for many years, he cut the number of daily homework problems to four. As a part of each day's homework, in place of the fifth problem, he gave students the following directions:

Choose any one of the four problems in this set that you have already solved. Explain and document, step-by-step, in complete and grammatical sentences, exactly how you solved that problem. Be prepared to lead the class through your solution in our next session.

At first, several of the students balked at doing an ungraded, noncredit assessment exercise that seemed to have more to do with writing skills than with calculus. The instructor quickly decided to offer students credit for doing the assessment exercise equal to that they would have received for the fifth homework problem. For a detailed, thoughtfully documented, well-written response, students got full credit. For a slapdash, *pro forma* response, on the other hand, they received no credit.

He still refrained from grading the assessments, however, limiting himself to writing a comment, suggestion, or question in the margin. The students' documented problem solutions gave him many insights into how and where students got stuck, or took "wrong turns" in their problem solving approaches. Being able to see students' thinking processes reflected in their writing gave the instructor many opportunities to diagnose and treat problems more effectively and to praise good strategies more clearly.

In class, he called on individual students to talk through their solutions to specific homework problems. Each time a student picked up the chalk and demonstrated a solution, he or she was forced to become an active participant. Instead of demonstrating solutions as students took notes—which he had come to see as doing the work for them—the instructor was able to act as a learning "coach," providing students with valuable practice in problem solving and helping them when they got stuck or off-track.

After about a month of documenting problem solutions, nearly all the students in his calculus class became relatively skilled at explaining the steps they had taken. They also greatly improved their ability to identify where they ran into difficulties in problems they failed to solve. By focusing on and assessing their problem solving skills, the calculus instructor found he had helped students better learn them.

ASSESSING CONDITIONAL LEARNING

In Physics

To gauge and improve students' understanding of the applications of physics to the life sciences, this instructor began taking time every third or fourth class session to ask students to fill out an Applications Card.[7] Specifically, he handed out index cards, then asked students to jot down as many applications as they could of the topic they had been studying—for example, elasticity, viscosity, or heat conduction—to the life sciences. He then collected the Applications Cards responses, sorted them into realistic and unrealistic or mistaken applications, and prepared his summary.

At the beginning of the next class, he shared, via overhead transparencies, four or five different realistic applications and praised their anonymous authors. He next presented a couple of unrealistic or off-target responses, slightly altered to disguise them from their authors, and asked the class to figure out why they weren't acceptable. As the weeks went on, students got noticeably better at generating creative, realistic applications of physics principles to life sciences. He also noticed that students became more interested and engaged in learning physics as they saw its applications to their majors and future careers.

ASSESSING REFLECTIVE LEARNING

In Environmental Studies

To assess her students' views on nuclear energy before they began reading and discussing that energy source, and to encourage them to personalize the issues involved, this professor used a simple, anonymous Classroom Opinion Poll.[7] Among the five questions she included was the following:

Assuming I have a choice, if changing my lifestyle would help make constructing more nuclear power plants unnecessary, I'd (circle one response):

    a. Not be willing to use less electrical energy or pay more for it
    b. Be willing to use much less electrical energy but not pay more for it
    c. Use the same amount of energy but be willing to pay a higher price for
      it
    d. Be willing to use much less energy and pay a higher price for it

After tallying the responses, she presented them to the class and led a discussion on the relationships among personal preferences, choices, and values and environmental policy.

ASSESSING METACOGNITIVE LEARNING

In Biology

Having taught introductory biology for several years, this professor was well aware of the difficulties students typically had in understanding metabolism. In an attempt to discover better ways to teach the topic, she asked students to fill out Diagnostic Learning Logs.[7] These forms consisted of a series of questions that required students to document how and how much they had studied, to reflect on what they had understood and what they had not, and to list steps they had taken when they did not understand.

From skimming these anonymous, one-page responses to the Diagnostic Learning Logs, the biology professor determined that students were stymied by the density of the text and the unfamiliar vocabulary, and that they were unable to figure out how to tell the main points from the details. A few students clearly had successful strategies for overcoming these roadblocks, so she shared those with the class during the next meeting and suggested a number of other ways to study and to monitor their studying more effectively.

COSTS AND BENEFITS OF CLASSROOM ASSESSMENT

From 1988 to 1991, the Pew Memorial Trust and the Ford Foundation jointly funded the Classroom Research Project. K. Patricia Cross directed the project, and I served as assistant director in this effort to develop and disseminate Classroom Assessment. After two years of working closely with faculty groups on a half-dozen college campuses, we surveyed experienced participants in the Classroom Research Project to explore teachers' views on the costs and benefits of using Classroom Assessment.

The Costs of Participating in Classroom Assessment

The three most frequently mentioned "costs" were, respectively: time required, sacrifice of some content coverage, and frustration when closure is not reached.

Time

Classroom Assessment takes faculty time. No matter how simple the Classroom Assessment Technique used, some out-of-class faculty time is required to plan the assessment, analyze feedback, and prepare a response. It also takes time, when teachers are collaborating, to discuss Classroom Assessment experiences with colleagues. And it takes time in class to administer the CAT, collect feedback, and to respond to student feedback. Time is the faculty's most precious resource, so any time required is a cost.

Content Coverage

Many faculty also felt that they were able to "cover less content" as a result of using Classroom Assessment. This was only partly because of the time needed to administer and respond to the CATs, however. The most important reason faculty gave for covering less content was that the assessments had convinced them of the need to review, revisit, or reteach important material not learned well enough. Most said that before using CATs, they would simply have gone on. But faced with feedback indicating inadequate learning, they chose to respond. Even when faculty felt sure that they had taught somewhat less, but taught it better, they still regretted the loss of content "coverage."

Lack of Closure

The third cost is related to the fact that Classroom Assessments often raise more questions about student learning than they answer. Teachers sometimes commented that they could have spent a week pondering their students' responses to a single assessment question because the data were so rich. But time and the pressure to cover material kept them moving. Student responses are sometimes puzzling, or even opaque. One Classroom Assessment question has a tendency to lead to another. And a response that works well for one class may not work at all the following semester—even in the same course. Faculty noted this paucity of final answers, or lack of closure, as the third major cost of participating in Classroom Research.

The Benefits of Participating in Classroom Assessment

The participants in campus Classroom Assessment programs were quite clear that the benefits of engaging in this approach far outweighed the costs. The three most frequently mentioned benefits of participation are explained below.

Collegiality

The single most frequently mentioned benefit of Classroom Assessment was one neither Professor Cross nor I would have predicted. Over and over again, faculty participants said that they benefited most from meeting and working with other colleagues. They valued the opportunities provided by on-campus Classroom Assessment programs to engage in clearly focused discussions on teaching and learning with colleagues and to collaborate on projects aimed at understanding and improving the quality of student learning. While faculty can practice Classroom Assessment independently and in isolation, most have not. Instead, many of those who have enjoyed the greatest success with Classroom Assessment have been members of campus groups.

Positive Student Response

Many faculty are unprepared for the enthusiasm with which students respond to their requests for feedback on their learning. When the students know that data are being gathered to help them learn better, and not simply to grade them, they are usually not only willing, but anxious to participate in Classroom Assessments. Many faculty have reported higher levels of student-faculty interaction and more active classroom participation as outcomes. It appears that most students enjoy and appreciate responding to Classroom Assessments *if* the instructor makes the purpose and outcomes of the assessments explicit and clearly uses the results to improve classroom learning.

Intellectual Excitement and Renewal

Most of the participants in our project were veteran faculty members, professors at mid-career or beyond. Most of them were also teaching in institutions where there were relatively few opportunities or incentives to carry out traditional disciplinary assessment. Many of these experienced college teachers found a new outlet for their intellectual energies in Classroom Assessment. They spoke of being "revitalized" and "challenged" by the opportunities this approach afforded them to apply their disciplinary inquiry skills to follow-up questions about teaching and learning in their courses.

Professor Cross and I were fascinated to observe that the benefits faculty ascribe to Classroom Assessment were, in many ways, mirror-images of the costs. For example, although faculty often complained that meeting with their fellow Classroom Researchers cost them time, those same teachers overwhelmingly endorsed their interaction with colleagues as the most important benefit. The benefits of making time to talk about their projects outweighed the costs, but the costs were still real. And it was student responses to the CATs, and their active engagement in the process, that most often convinced faculty to trade off some breadth of coverage for more depth in learning. To complete the ironic parallelism, the flip side of the ultimately unfinishable and unpredictable nature of Classroom Assessment that frustrated some faculty is the open-ended, dynamic quality that others valued as a source of intellectual excitement.

Classroom Assessment requires limited faculty time or effort, and demands no specialized technical skills. Classroom Assessment greatly increases the probability that information collected about teaching and learning will actually be used to improve teaching and learning. It also allows the individual faculty member to control the assessment process and the information that results. As a consequence, it poses few real or perceived risks to college faculty.

GUIDELINES FOR SUCCESS

The following five suggestions for successful Classroom Assessment represent more lessons learned from faculty involved in the original funded project.

1. Keep it simple and short. Don't make Classroom Assessment into a self-inflicted chore or burden. Limit the amount of time, in and out of class, that you will invest. Collect only as much data as you can turn into information.
2. Keep it focused. While there are many interesting questions you might ask, focus on those most likely to improve achievement of essential course goals. Make sure students understand the purpose and promise of the assessment.
3. Don't ask if you don't want to know, or won't be able to respond. Assessing and then not responding, or responding badly to student feedback, is usually more damaging than not assessing at all.
4. Make sure your aim is true. Try your Classroom Assessment Technique out on yourself and a colleague before you use it in class. Questions, directions, and exercises need to be as clear and unambiguous as possible.
5. Close the feedback loop. Make sure to let students know the outcomes of the assessment and what changes those outcomes suggest for you and them.

CONCLUSION

While there are many effective techniques for involving students actively in their learning,[9,10] activity by itself does not guarantee learning quality. To get the most from investing in active instruction, faculty need to monitor and provide feedback on student learning. Classroom Assessment is one simple, low-risk method for doing just that. In addition to providing teachers with information they can use to adjust instruction, Classroom Assessment has the added advantage of actively involving students in assessing and improving their own learning. As such, it is one means college teachers can use to improve the quality of higher learning in the life sciences where that improvement matters most—in our classrooms and in the minds of our students.

REFERENCES

1. MAJUMDAR, S. K., et al., Eds. 1991. Science Education in the United States: Issues, Crisis, and Priorities. The Pennsylvania Academy of Science. Easton, PA.

2. RIGDEN, J. S. & S. TOBIAS. 1991. Tune in, turn off, drop out: Why so many college students abandon science after the introductory courses. The Sciences **31(1):** 16–20.
3. SEYMOUR, E. 1992. 'The Problem Iceberg' in science, mathematics, and engineering education: Student explanations for high attrition rates. J. Coll. Sci. Teaching **21(4):** 230–237.
4. SEYMOUR, E. 1992. Undergraduate problems with teaching and advising in SME majors—Explaining gender differences in attrition rates. J. Coll. Sci. Teaching **21(5):** 284–292.
5. PASCARELLA, E. T. & P. T. TERENZINI. 1991. How College Affects Students: Findings and Insights from Twenty Years of Research. Jossey-Bass. San Francisco, CA.
6. CROSS, K. P. "What's in that Black Box?," or, How Do We Know What Students are Learning (p. 4). Howard R. Bowen Lecture at the Claremont Graduate School, November 8, 1989. Claremont, CA.
7. ANGELO, T. A. & K. P. CROSS. 1993. Classroom Assessment Techniques: A Handbook for College Teachers. (2nd ed.). Jossey-Bass. San Francisco, CA.
8. ANGELO, T. A. 1991. Ten easy pieces: Assessing higher learning in four dimensions. *In* Classroom Research: Early Lessons from Success. T. A. Angelo, Ed. New Directions for Teaching and Learning, No. 46. Jossey-Bass. San Francisco, CA.
9. BONWELL. C. C. & J. A. EISON. 1991. Active Learning: Creating Excitement in the Classroom. ASHE-ERIC Higher Education Report, No. 1. The George Washington University, School of Education and Human Development. Washington, DC.
10. MEYERS, C. & T. B. JONES. 1993. Promoting Active Learning: Stretegies for the College Classroom. Jossey-Bass. San Francisco, CA.

Designing Process-oriented Learning Resources

KATHLEEN McDERMOTT HANNAFIN[a]

Center for Educational Excellence and
Department of Behavioral Science and Leadership
United States Air Force Academy
USAF Academy, Colorado 80840

During the last 20 years, researchers and educators have focused great interest and effort on designing and developing learning resources which facilitate student thinking, critical reasoning, problem solving skills, and ability to connect and transform information into new understandings. Many of these efforts have focused on development of student thinking processes. This paper describes one means of designing such resources.

OVERVIEW OF PROCESS-ORIENTED LEARNING RESOURCES

Definition

For the purposes of this paper, process-oriented resources are defined as teaching and learning activities which engage students cognitively in analyzing and transforming information.[1] These resources enrich student thinking processes, enhance end-performance, and facilitate connected understandings.

Cognitive Engagement

Process-oriented resources promote cognitive engagement by requiring students to invoke specific cognitive functions and operations. These functions and operations orient students to new information, facilitate retrieval of related information from long-term memory, construct and transform information, and encode new understandings into long-term memory.[2,3] For example, cognitively orienting students to a new learning task may be accomplished by requiring students to examine (e.g., look at) a dataset. During examination, patterns and relationships among and between various data points may be observed. Initially orienting the students to the task and then requiring them to focus their thinking and observing processes demands cognitive engagement and invocation of specific cognitive functions. This is a processes-oriented view of learning which is also student-centered. That is, teaching and learning are viewed from the perspective of student processes needed to learn and develop insight.

[a]Present address: 2019 Middlewood Drive, Tallahassee, Florida 32312.

Knowledge Reconstruction

Process-oriented resources induce specific cognitive functions, such as orienting, retrieving, and processing, in order to acquire, then reconstruct knowledge. For example, requiring students to generate lists of similarities and differences between and among biophysical systems induces many cognitive processes. Next have students compare, contrast, and revise understandings to orient their thinking, retrieve specific mental models of similarities and differences from long-term memory, actively process (think about, generate written descriptions, etc.) critical attributes, and finally restructure their knowledge (prior understandings) in order to develop new insights. Such activities promote reconstruction of basic knowledge and the formation of new insights and deeper understandings.

Resource Options

Process-oriented learning resources range in complexity and diversity. They may be designed as complete teaching and learning systems, such as medical or trauma simulators; as a single teaching method, for example, inquiry-based teaching or modeling of problem solving strategies; or as individual learning activities, such as manipulation of data to see effects on various functions and processes. Resources may be technology-based—courseware, computer-based lessons; designed for specific classrooms—laboratories, for example; or for individuals or groups, for instance, cooperative and collaborative case study activities.

Teaching Methodologies

Process-oriented learning resources need to be supported by compatible process-oriented teaching methods. That is, if process-oriented outcomes are desired—critical thinking, reasoning, problem-solving—then teaching methods which model and require the application of these processes must be employed. This is not the same as instructing in specific problem solving procedures. If one merely provides repeated practice in solving problems, students will supply whatever underlying thinking processes they already have. If those processes are faulty or inefficient, students may, by chance, solve problems successfully, but never develop insight or understanding into general problem solving strategies.

Teaching rigid procedural approaches tends to promote rigid, "by the numbers" procedures for solving problems; when a procedure can be applied mechanically, little insight is available to free process itself. For example, many students are given "cookbook" steps to follow when solving certain types of equations. While these "steps" can be followed to solve many problems, often students attend more to application of steps than to developing understanding of why the steps are applied. As a result, they "go through the motions" but never develop the insight to solve problems in general. On the other hand, teachers can verbalize, describe, and model their thinking processes for students. Students model not only how an expert solves problems, but also the reasoning processes underlying the processes. This is a potent process, where the teacher acts as a process resource, modeling planned and systematic processes for students and describing the systematic methods used to analyze, question, manipulate and solve problems. Intentional or prototypical "mistakes" may used to illustrate, demonstrate, or test the effects of faulty logic and hypotheses. This approach is different from mastery instruction, where teachers provide steps or require students to memorize and then apply steps to solve problems. Without explaining the underlying rationale of the problem solving process, thinking strategies are unlikely to develop. Through active modeling, students are able to model the processes directly, modify the observed process, or compare and contrast their own thinking with expert processes.

GUIDELINES FOR DEVELOPING
PROCESS-ORIENTED RESOURCES

Six basic steps are recommended: determine desired student outcomes; evaluate alternative teaching and learning processes to be utilized; assess the cognitive requirements of outcomes; define the scope of the resource; develop methods for integrating teaching, learning, and resource design; and develop methods for assessing and evaluating the resources.

1. Determine Desired Student Outcomes

A description of the desired student outcomes must be generated; that is, what students should understand after completing or utilizing the resources. Unlike traditional behavioral objectives, resource outcomes emphasize higher-level reasoning processes. If broad understandings of scientific principles are desired, then outcomes reflecting critical analysis of data and the formulation of hypotheses may be warranted. Designers must conceptualize the outcomes, then operationalize the underlying cognitive operations which are needed to achieve the processes. For example, if desired outcomes include relating new information to prior knowledge (retrieving), examining data (orienting), formulating and testing hypotheses (structuring and processing), then both teaching and learning activities must be implemented. The means to attain these outcomes can also be described (for example, a written laboratory journal which requires students to describe and explain their thinking, prior understandings, and personal experience, regarding the data, observations made, and hypotheses formulated). This design step extends the traditional notion of outcomes beyond strict behavioral measures and causes both the student and teacher to focus on underlying thought processes.

2. Evaluate Alternative Pedagogical and Learning Processes

Examine pedagogical beliefs which you believe facilitate and underlie successful teacher processes and student learning. This examination is a reflective process which requires the designer to consider both the view of the learner and the teacher. Beliefs drive the design process by providing a theoretical framework, a research base, and a rationale for design decisions. Additional examination assists in classifying design decisions as active or passive, didactic or process, inquiry or discovery, and so forth. Further refinement of beliefs assists in describing the methods to be used by teachers and the processes students need to invoke during learning. Without an understanding of the underlying (pedagogical and learning) processes, resources may evolve but they will lack congruency and purpose.

3. Assess Cognitive Requirements

Next, determine the cognitive activities of the desired student outcomes. This examination should reveal a clear understanding of the cognitive functions and operations required of students to transform, construct, or reconstruct their knowledge. The requirements should be further refined and classified as to whether they require active or passive student engagement (for example, note-taking, listening, following teacher directions versus constructing, generating, and testing student hypotheses); and active or passive teaching methods (for example, lecturing, restating, or listing procedures versus building contexts for understanding, prompting for understanding via probing questions, or creating dissonance in student perspectives). This activity clarifies teaching methods, operational definition of outcomes, and provides guidance for determining assessment and evaluation methods.

4. Define Scope of Resource

As stated previously, learning resources range in diversity and complexity. To mention a few, they can be designed as tools for enhancing understanding (e.g., analogs/extenders), particular teaching methods (e.g., modeling processes), and course or lesson activities. In this practical design step, resource specifications and requirements are determined as well as the human and financial resources required to produce the resource. Operationalizing and testing the resource is an additional consideration when determining the scope of the resource to be developed.

5. Develop Methods for Integrating Teaching, Learning, and Resource Design

Often, learning resources are designed in a piecemeal fashion, focusing on a single facet of teaching and learning, such as improving content understanding or refining a set of curriculum materials. Resources developed in isolation from, and without regard for, the underlying teaching methods, desired process outcomes, or assessment methods utilized lack consistency in design and purpose.

One method for preventing this piecemeal approach is to develop a particular teaching "scheme." A teaching scheme requires all design decisions (teaching, learning, and assessment methods) to reflect a set of unifying pedagogical beliefs. Schemes function to organize teaching and learning within a common frame of reference, mental model, or orientation. They provide the underlying foundation for all development activities and design decisions. Many contemporary learning resources are designed with underlying teaching schemes, such as situated cognition (Jasper Series),[4] computer-based microworlds,[5] context-based learning,[6] connectionism,[7] and metaphor.[8]

6. Develop Methods for Assessing and Evaluating Resources

Process-oriented learning resources require assessment and evaluation methods consistent with the adopted teaching methods and desired learning outcomes. Methods need to assess the development of student thinking skills as well as the acquisition and integration of new knowledge. Assessment and evaluation are often a combination of traditional and nontraditional methods. Methods will differ from traditional methods in that they assess the manner in which students have restructured knowledge, their solving of unfamiliar problems, and their critical treatment of topics and issues.

Changes in thinking cannot be assessed using a single indicator or at single point in time, for example, a multiple choice test or a single essay. Because process thinking develops as any other skill over time, assessment data must be taken over time in order to document the development of thinking skills. Additionally, multiple data sources should be employed to allow teachers to examine and guide student thinking.

Assessment methods which require students to externalize their internal understanding of both content and processes of learning can be gathered over time and through various means. Written records (e.g., journals, laboratory chronicles) are one method of assessing student ability to think critically about problems. Through written entries, the teacher observes development of both breadth and depth of knowledge. Additionally, written assignments afford opportunity for students to demonstrate the connectedness of new understandings by relating prior knowledge, stating points of view, or describing alternative perspectives on problems, questions, and possible solutions. Portfolios of written work, collected throughout the semester, can also be employed to assess and evaluate process-oriented teaching and learning activities.

CONCLUSION

Designing and developing process-oriented learning resources requires an active teaching style, a willingness to restructure many traditional classroom activities, and a willingness to analyze students' thinking processes and skills. Instructors must understand, be aware of, and plan teaching methods based on the cognitive processing required of students. Additionally, teachers must insure a balance between acquisition of content knowledge and acquisition of critical supporting processes which enable learning.

This paper does not reflect easy solutions for improving teaching and learning, but offers only thoughtful methods for making improvements. Designing process-oriented learning resources does not differ in many ways from traditional resources, in that they require hard work, both mental and physical. Hopefully, new resources will yield improvements in teaching and learning and create opportunities to enhance student learning.

SUMMARY

During the last two decades great effort has been dedicated to improving undergraduate education. Often, traditional instructional methods have been criticized as being passive, overly prescriptive, and concerned with discrete, disconnected measures of student performance.[9] Contemporary research in cognitive psychology as well as in teaching and learning offers promise for expanding traditional notions for design of educational resources and have yielded new methods for resource improvement. This paper has described one method for improvement: design of process-oriented learning resources.

REFERENCES

1. Solso, R. L. Cognitive Psychology, 3rd ed.: 521. Simon & Schuster. Needham Heights. MA.
2. Hooper, R. & M. J. Hannafin. 1988. Learning the ROPES of instructional design: Guidelines of emerging interactive technologies. Educ. Technol. 28(7): 14–18.
3. Hannafin, M. J. & L. P. Reiber. 1989. Psychological foundations of instructional design for emerging computer-based instructional technologies. Educ. Technol. Res. Dev. 37: 91–114.
4. The Cognition and Technology Group at Vanderbilt. 1990. Anchored Instruction and its relationship to situated cognition. Educ. Researcher August-September 1990: 2–10.
5. diSessa, A. 1983. Phenomonology and the evolution of intuition. In Mental Models, D. Gentner & A. L. Stevens, Eds.: 267–298. Erlbaum Associates. Hillsdale, NJ.
6. Wheatley, G. H. 1990. Spatial Sense and Mathematics Learning. Arithmetic Teacher. February 1990: 10–11.
7. Bereiter, C. 1991. Implications of connectionism for thinking about rules. Educ. Researcher. April 1991: 10–16.
8. Stepich, D. A. & T. J. Newby. 1988. Analogical instruction within the information processing paradigm: Effective means to facilitate learning. Instructional Sci. 17: 129–144.
9. Schuell, T. J. 1986. Cognitive conceptions of Learning. Rev. Educ. Res. 56(4): 411–436.

Life Science Education: Reflections on Some Challenges Facing Us

JOEL A. MICHAEL[a] AND HAROLD I. MODELL[b,c]

[a]Department of Physiology
Rush Medical College
Chicago, Illinois 60612

[b]National Resource for Computers in Life Science Education
P.O. Box 51187
Seattle, Washington 98115

The goal of this workshop was to enable participants to explore possible roles in helping students become intellectually active learners in the life science classroom. The individual formats of specific sessions varied, some having been designed to have participants (1) assume the role of students in a physiology class, (2) assume the role of faculty engaged in planning sessions involving active learning, or (3) interact with the session leader as colleagues involved in life science education. Thus, open discussion was encouraged, and issues related to the specific techniques being demonstrated, the educational environments in which participants work, and common concerns of most participants (regardless of their educational environments) were explored.

The workshop was recorded and transcribed so that common questions and issues, whether arising in formal presentations or in informal sessions, could be addressed explicitly in this volume. Our goal for this summary is to articulate those concerns and problems that were most frequently voiced by the participants and to at least attempt to address them. We do this, not because we believe that we are able to propose appropriate solutions for all of the challenges facing us, but rather because the first step toward identifying solutions is to understand the questions.

When reviewing the transcripts of the workshop, we were impressed that, although the group represented faculty from a variety of life science departments in diverse educational environments (community college through medical school), common themes appeared and reappeared throughout the discussions. These fell into four broad categories: (1) faculty as teachers; (2) students as learners; (3) the "curriculum," or what we teach and how we do it; and (4) the learning resources available to support our efforts.

FACULTY AS TEACHERS

Most teachers of the life sciences in higher education are, in a real sense, "accidental teachers." That is, they entered their particular discipline because of

[c]To whom correspondence should be addressed.

an interest in the scientific aspects of the discipline rather than a specific interest in teaching. Future faculty are trained in increasingly narrow subspecialties and forced to maintain a narrow focus in order to stay competitive in the research community. They receive little or no training, either as graduate students or as junior faculty, directed towards their effectiveness as teachers. Furthermore, many faculty members feel as if they are working in isolation, with few, if any, opportunities to share and learn from the teaching experiences of colleagues. The final "insult" is that there are still relatively few rewards for involvement in and success at teaching! The impact of these factors on life science education raises the following questions that must be addressed if significant progress is to be made.

- What training should graduate students in life science disciplines receive in teaching methods, and how should that training be organized and offered?
- How can we create faculty development opportunities for faculty, particularly junior faculty? How can we help faculty whose research efforts necessitate a narrow focus to broaden their focus as teachers?
- How can we encourage change in the academic community so that effective teaching is rewarded appropriately?
- How can we most effectively create a community of life science educators, both locally, at our individual institutions, and globally?

Learning new skills requires an active process. This is true whether the skills are related to physiological problem solving or to effective teaching. Graduate students need exposure to some didactic presentation about effective teaching methods, but there is also a great need for opportunities to practice those methods with appropriate feedback from more expert teachers. Junior faculty, as they strive to become educators, need the same kind of feedback about their performance. Faculty development, then, should be an ongoing process, beginning during the years of graduate training, accelerating as a junior faculty member, and continuing as one's career develops and matures.

It is not clear how this can be accomplished. Any significant effort in this area requires support by resources that are currently in short supply. Equally important, however, is the willingness of life scientists to participate in this process. For many faculty, this will require a change in the culture of academia (at least the scientific side of it) and a change in reward structures. There has been some suggestion in the past few years that changes in these areas are taking place. The recent decrease in availability of research funds may help refocus priorities in the life science academic community. Only time will tell whether significant changes will result from these and other external factors (e.g., the growing movement for academic accountability).

If, indeed, teaching and educational development come to be viewed as "scholarly" efforts and are rewarded as such, it is reasonable to assume that some faculty will reassess the focus of their academic efforts. We could then expect to see the development of a broad-based community of life science teachers. Certainly, a major portion of the faculty population will continue to direct their primary efforts toward their various scientific research endeavors, although they may also expend some of the energy they currently direct toward "basic science" research on activities directed toward improving life science education. At the other extreme will be those faculty whose primary responsibility is teaching, although they, too, may be involved in efforts aimed at improving life science education. As a result, a "community" of life scientists devoted to life science education may evolve. However, for this community to develop, it is essential that the faculty view their educational efforts in the same light as they did their basic science research efforts. That is, they must communicate their efforts to their peers. In recent years, the number of forums for communicating about life science education has increased. In the realm of physiology, for example, the American Physiological Society (APS) now has a formal section devoted to the teaching of physiology. The Teaching of Physiology Section sponsors symposia, workshops, poster-discussion sessions, and other forums at the annual meeting of the APS. In addition, the APS is publishing a journal, a section of the *American Journal of Physiology* entitled *Advances in Physiology Education,* to provide a mechanism for publishing peer-reviewed papers related to physiology education at all academic levels. Another recent communication forum for anatomy and physiology faculty is the Human Anatomy and Physiology Society.

One final issue needs to be addressed. With the progress in biomedical science has come increasing specialization of training. One is no longer a "physiologist" or even a "cardiovascular physiologist"; today, one is an expert on central nervous system regulation of cardiovascular function or a specialist in cardiac muscle energetics. The same is true in biochemistry, biology, microbiology, and, essentially, all other life science disciplines. As a consequence, it is increasingly difficult for researchers to teach subjects even slightly afield from their respective areas of specialization and particularly difficult for such individuals to be effective in communicating the broad concepts that are so important for our students to master. To the extent that we can succeed at creating a life science education community, a group of people who share ideas, we will each be able to broaden ourselves more readily to become more effective teachers.

STUDENTS AS LEARNERS

During the course of the workshop, questions were raised concerning the effect of student attitudes on the success of an active learning environment. Our students have grown up in an academic environment in which faculty provide a body of information to the class. Tests are designed to assess how well this body of information has been assimilated, and grades are generally assigned on the basis of a curve on which only a limited number of students can receive the highest grade. As a result, students expect to operate in a highly competitive atmosphere in which excellence is judged on the basis of the extent of an acquired database. If we are to be successful in fostering an environment in which students are intellectually active and are concerned not with acquiring a large database, but rather with learning how to use available information to solve problems, we must address the following questions.

- How can we get students to take responsibility for their own learning and become "active" learners?
- How can we foster a cooperative rather than a competitive learning environment?
- How can we foster intellectual curiosity in students?
- How can we reshape students attitudes so that faculty is viewed as facilitators of learning rather than disseminators of knowledge?

The key to the answers to these questions lies in bringing about a better match between student expectations and the expectations of an active learning environment. Although it is clear that students differ considerably in their preferred learning styles, it is also clear that the behaviors and expectations of the teacher have a significant impact on the way students view learning. The reason why students expect their courses to be based on fact intake–recall is that, in their experience, most courses have been conducted in that way. Thus, the first step is to make the faculty's expectations for the course clear. The faculty must then conduct the course in a way that is consistent with the stated expectations. In addition, if we want students to become active learners, we must help them understand what we mean by the term, active learning, and we must provide them with a model of this behavior.

Thus, we help students take responsibility for their own learning by establishing criteria and conducting our courses in a way that requires them to do so. We can change the students' current view of the faculty by publicly redefining the faculty's role as that of facilitator and ensuring that, in executing the course, the faculty behave in this way. Designing course activities with this in mind can also help students develop collegial attitudes about their learning. Curriculum design can also play an important role in fostering cooperative rather than competitive learning environments (see discussion below).

Finally, we can foster student intellectual curiosity by designing course activities to illustrate and emphasize that the course material is relevant to their personal lives and their personal view of the world. In doing so, we must demonstrate that the skills that we want them to develop are useful, not only in their pursuit of the life sciences, but also in many other aspects of their everyday lives. We must not become so tightly focused on the specific content of our course or our curriculum that we lose sight of the more general relevance of what we do and what we want our students to be able to do.

THE CURRICULUM: WHAT WE TEACH
AND HOW WE TEACH IT

Perhaps the most vigorous discussion centered around the apparent conflict between teaching "content" and promoting active learning. In part, this conflict hinges on a common, but unnecessarily narrow, definition of teaching as imparting information (i.e., lecturing). If promoting active learning means that less content can be included in "lecture" time, will students learn the necessary content? Obviously, one's answer to this question depends on how and what has been established as the necessary content. In a wide variety of educational settings, what one teaches is, at least partially, constrained by the need to prepare students for external, standardized examinations, either the Medical College Admissions Test (the MCAT exam) or the National Board of Medical Examiners ("National Boards"). These considerations tend to lead to curriculum design based on the question, "What do the students need to know upon completion of the course (or curriculum)?"

An alternative approach is to design a performance- or outcome-based curriculum focused on the question, "What skills should the students develop and how can they apply those skills upon completion of the course (or curriculum)?" This approach also requires definition of a content base for each academic level, but it goes beyond the focus of many of today's curricula in that it puts a stated emphasis on *utilizing* a knowledge base rather than merely *acquiring* a knowledge base.

These possibilities, along with the impact of curricular design on issues related to the student as a learner, lead to the following curricular questions for the life science community.

- What is the appropriate content for courses offered to bioscience majors, and how should we go about defining it?
- What is the appropriate content for courses offered to non-bioscience majors or non-science majors?
- What problem solving skills do we expect our students to master? What do we expect them to be able to "do" with the content they acquire?
- How can we design our courses in a way that will promote active learning and the achievement of our objectives in classrooms with large and growing numbers of students?
- How should we define and assess student achievement if memorized content is no longer an essential objective for our courses?
- How do we assist our "unconverted" colleagues to accept the need for such change, and how do we assist them to actually make the needed changes?

Most current curricula are instructor-based rather than student-centered. The myth of the "indispensability of the lecturer" is a pervasive one. There seems to be an overriding assumption that if "we" (the teachers) don't say "it" in class, the students won't learn "it." Furthermore, if the primary goal of our course is to ensure that the students "get" all of "it," we must mention all of "it" in class, lest we fail in reaching our objectives.

We must combat this myth, and there are several germane arguments with which to counter it. First, it is simply not true that saying it in class ensures that students will learn it. Learning is not an infectious process, and words wafting through the air of the classroom do not lodge in the brains of the audience and constitute learning. Even when memorization occurs on such exposure, its longevity is minimal, usually until the next test is administered. Meaningful learning requires something more than passive reception of the lecturer's words!

Furthermore, even if content could be memorized and retained by simple exposure in class, it would still constitute inert knowledge, knowledge that the student cannot use or apply in solving problems. The acquisition of such knowledge is surely the epitome of an "academic" exercise, one with no point beyond the earning of a grade.

The myth of the lecturer also takes responsibility for learning away from the student and gives it to the lecturer. This is a critical error, for, in order to be successful in their chosen life paths, students must take responsibility for their learning and engage in the process of self-learning. An educational diet of nothing but lecture is the surest way to defeat the development of self-learners.

Perhaps the best argument against this myth is the fact that students continue to expand their knowledge base long after the course is completed. Indeed, by the time the life science student completes his or her degree, the knowledge base relevant to many topics covered during his or her formal coursework has expanded considerably. Thus, not only is the notion that all relevant content must be presented in class flawed from a learning standpoint, the content deemed relevant for a given course changes from year to year.

The issues with which we should be concerned, then, are (1) defining the content necessary at a particular level that will allow students to develop and apply the skills appropriate for that level and (2) determining how faculty can help students develop and apply those skills. Taking this approach, the perspective changes from the instructor "passing on" information to the students learning to use information with the help of the instructor. Assessment of student achievement becomes a performance-based process aimed at determining whether the students' skill levels are appropriate for the particular academic level.

Adopting this view also has implications for modifying student attitudes and fostering the type of cooperative learning that must take place in a collegial community.

LEARNING RESOURCES TO SUPPORT ACTIVE LEARNING

The final topic that generated considerable discussion was the availability of appropriate learning resources that can be used to support active learning and problem solving. Although the content area upon which most of this discussion was focused was physiology, the issues raised are relevant to all life science areas. The discussion revolved around the following questions.

- What is the role of the textbook in today's educational environment and do textbooks aimed at different academic levels play the same role?
- What should textbooks contain?
- What other resources are available to help foster an active learning environment, and how can we learn about them?

The traditional role of life science textbooks has been that of a repository of current information. The difference between texts covering the same general topic but aimed at different academic levels has been the degree of detail included. In recent years, as more cognitive science data related to the way in which students learn has become available, the overall format of textbooks has changed, particularly at the undergraduate level. Recent undergraduate physiology books, for example, include more conceptual aids to help students construct analogies and mental models of physiological systems. A recent undergraduate anatomy and physiology text contains a section devoted to constructing concept maps as a way of organizing information, and the book includes sample concept maps for various systems of the body. Hence, the role seems to be changing, at least at the undergraduate level, from a source of information to a learning tool.

Unfortunately, textbooks at the professional (e.g., medical, graduate) level have not evolved in this direction. New editions of texts that originally appeared over 30 years ago have been updated to contain the latest factual information and interpretation of that information, but they retain the same format and philosophy with regard to the student use of the resource. Perhaps it is time that we rethink how texts are used in the curriculum. The issues range from the format and style of the book to the amount of factual detail included and the degree to which the factual detail is referenced.

If we are to emphasize an active intellectual exercise for students, the written materials that we provide as a supplement to classroom activities should reflect this overall philosophy and assist the student in engaging in these types of exercises. The question then becomes whether the text should contain only enough factual content to develop the concepts presented or whether the text should also serve as a reference for future study.

These are multifaceted issues whose resolution most likely includes a spectrum of approaches. Nevertheless, if the intent of textbook authors is to help students build mental models of the systems covered, they must consciously address them when designing their texts.

Textbooks, however, are not the only resource necessary to support an active learning environment. Activities in the form of "real" laboratory or technology-based exercises that encourage students to think about systems by generating and testing hypotheses are also needed. Although active learning through problem-based curricula has become a popular approach in life science education, workshop participants expressed some frustration about the paucity of available source books containing material that can be used as the basis for problem-based activities or serve as models for faculty wishing to develop problems tailored specifically to their student populations.

IN CLOSING

While planning for this workshop, we sought to attract an audience representative of the broad scope of life science education at a variety of academic levels, and we tried to produce a program that would stimulate discussion in the corridors as well as in the formal sessions. We believe that the workshop achieved these goals. The audience was large enough and broad enough in its disciplinary and institutional affiliations to produce an intellectual critical mass. As a result, the discussions were lively and wide ranging. While it is clear that there is still much to be done to reform life science education, it is clear that there is a cadre of interested, involved, and committed colleagues willing to participate in the effort. When the struggle becomes discouraging, it is important to remember that progress has been made and will continue to be made as a result of efforts by this dedicated group of life science educators. The challenge is to continue the dialogue within and between life science disciplines, for it is this type of discourse that leads to significant change.

Where To Find The Literature: An Annotated Bibliography of Sources for Life Science Education

JOEL A. MICHAEL

Department of Physiology
Rush Medical College
Chicago, Illinois 60612

One of the goals of this workshop was to contribute to the creation of a community of life science educators, a group of individuals sharing certain interests and communicating with one another. Scholarly communities characteristically interact through the published literature, and our community should be no different. But we life science teachers are part of still large communities dealing with science education, general education, and research in education.

Although the scholarly literature in life science education is still a relatively small one (although growing), the number of journals dealing with science education and general education is very large.

This annotated bibliography is intended to make available to the life science education community information about possible sources of ideas and inspiration as well as possible locations for our own communications. *This list is not exhaustive,* and even the largest university libraries do not subscribe to all of the journals listed here. Nevertheless, it is possible to gain access to this literature with only a little diligence.

Education Journals: Life Sciences

Advances in Physiology Education
Published by the American Physiological Society

The American Biology Teacher
Published by the National Association of Biology Teachers, Inc.

Journal of Biological Education
Published by the Institute of Biology (UK)

Biochemical Education
Published by the International Union of Biochemistry (UK)

These journals are of most obvious relevance to life science educators. They all publish on a broad range of topics from educational research to classroom applications.

Teaching and Learning in Medicine
Published by Lawrence Erlbaum Associates, Publishers

Medical Education
Published by the Association for the Study of Medical Education (U.K.)

The Medical Teacher
Carfax Publishing Company (U.K.)

These journals deal with the full range of issues in medical education, including considerable attention to teaching the basic sciences relevant to medicine (life sciences). Much of this is nonetheless applicable to life science education at all levels.

Education Journals: Other Sciences

Journal of Chemical Education
Published by the Division of Chemical Education of the American Chemical Society, Inc.

American Journal of Physics
The Physics Teacher
Published by the American Association of Physics Teachers

These are two excellent journals that publish educational and cognitive science research as well as articles dealing with the full range of classroom-related material. Their focus is on students from the high school level and beyond. A great deal of what is published here is directly relevant to the life science classroom.

Computers in Education Journals

Computers and Education
Pergamon Press PLC, Ltd.

Collegiate Microcomputer
Published by Rose-Hulman Institute of Technology

Journal of Educational Technology Systems
Baywood Publishing Co.

Journal of Computers in Mathematics and Science Teaching
Published by the Association for the Advancement of Computing in Education

Educational Technology
Educational Technology Publications, Inc.

These are but a few of the many journals publishing in the field of computer-based education. Articles on this subject also appear in many of the other journals listed here.

Research Journals: Science Education

Journal of Research in Science Teaching
Published by the National Association for Research in Science Teaching

Science Education
Published by John Wiley & Sons, Inc.

International Journal of Science Education
Published by Taylor & Francis (London)

These journals publish peer-reviewed research articles, reviews, theoretical discussions, etc., dealing with the teaching and learning of all science disciplines by students of all ages. Although only a fraction of the articles deals with the life sciences in any way, all of the papers are thought-provoking.

Research Journals: Education (General) and Cognitive Science

American Educational Research Journal
Review of Educational Research
Educational Research
Published by the American Educational Research Association

These journals published by AERA, the largest and broadest of the American groups concerned with educational research, deal with the full range of educational issues. As the need for reform of science education has become more evident, an increasing number of articles are appearing that deal with such issues.

Cognitive Science
Published by the Cognitive Science Society

Journal of the Learning Sciences
Published by Lawrence Erlbaum Associates.

Cognition and Instruction
Published by Lawrence Erlbaum Associates.

Instructional Science
Kluwer Academic Publishers Group

These journals publish research papers that report on studies of problem solving (most broadly defined) and learning from the cognitive science perspective. This research area is growing and developing rapidly and many of the ideas and theory being advanced are very relevant to the pursuit of active learning in the life science classroom.

Role Playing Facilitates Study of Clinical Cases by Large Groups

JOHN H. BECKER

Scholl College of Podiatric Medicine
1001 North Dearborn Street
Chicago, Illinois 60610

Many institutions continue to use large group teaching methods, such as lecturing, because of cost-effectiveness. However, small group sessions may enhance learning for many students. Therefore, instructors who are constrained to use large group settings may wish to utilize techniques having the advantages of small groups. One such method is the case study, used in business and professional education because it is more participatory, action-oriented and student-centered, and because it simulates the activity and problem solving of that profession. The method presented here is a variant of the case method, wherein volunteers from the student audience play small roles in the resolution of the case problem.

The case of a patient with muscular dystrophy is summarized on one page, including the clinical history and lab data, and given to the students one day in advance. From a class of 120 first-year medical students, volunteers are solicited in 14 pairs to play roles relevant to the case. Sample roles would be: biochemist, geneticist, podiatric physician, ethicist. On the day of presentation the moderator asks of each student pair three or four scripted questions relative to their role. At the end, the moderator summarizes the case and hands out a written case summary and an evaluative questionnaire.

Evaluations indicate that although only one-fifth of the class participated in a role, the format held the attention of the entire class. Students also liked the relaxed atmosphere, the comfort of being questioned in pairs, the requirement to think on their feet, and the problem-solving mode. A disadvantage is that the scripted questions do not allow pursuit of interesting digressions when time is limited. Nonetheless, Socratic questioning is typical of education in the clinics, and this case introduces first-year students to that style.

The student evaluations, and the author's own analysis of the utility of this case for three years of classes, lead to three conclusions. First, this case succeeds with a large group because the audience vicariously identifies with the smaller group of volunteer students. Secondly, role playing focuses their background research prior to presentation. Lastly, the roles themselves emphasize the interconnections between the basic and clinical sciences, and reinforces the team concept of medical care.

A Computer Method for Simulating Depolarization and Repolarization of Heart Ventricles for Use in Teaching the Electrocardiogram

JOHN D. BELL AND RICHARD W. HENINGER

Department of Zoology
Brigham Young University
Provo, Utah 84602

The teaching of time-dependent processes in physiology can be improved by the use of dynamic visual aids. Such is particularly true if the visual aid is designed to allow active participation by the students during the teaching process. We present here a computer simulation method to assist in teaching of the electrical properties of the heart ventricles and the electrocardiogram.

The computer program is designed to simulate and present visually the time-dependent depolarization and subsequent repolarization of the heart ventricles. The simulation is accomplished by dividing a two-dimensional graphical representation of the standard lead plane of the ventricles into 500 square sections or cells. An algorithm for the time-dependent voltage of a cardiac action potential is assigned to each cell. Initially, all the cells are assumed to be at resting membrane potential. The simulation initiates ventricular depolarization by starting the action potential sequence in one cell. At each segment of time in the sequence, the membrane potential of the rest of the cells is examined. Each time a cell becomes depolarized, the action potential sequence is initiated in the adjacent cells. The process is repeated until all of the cells have completed the sequence and returned to resting membrane potential. The sequence of depolarization and repolarization of the ventricles is presented graphically in the program by assigning a different color to each increment of membrane potential for each cell.

The measurement of the electrical field during the ventricular depolarization and repolarization for the electrocardiogram is simulated for each of the three standard limb leads as follows. The ventricles are divided into 21 equivalent regions arranged radially around the central point of the ventricular septum. The magnitude of the electrical dipole is calculated for each region. The component of that dipole in the direction of each of the standard leads is then determined based on the cosine of the angle between the region and the lead. Finally, the contributions of all the regions are summed for each lead to give the instantaneous potential relevant to that lead. When the simulation is completed, the computer program can plot the resulting electrocardiogram for each lead as well as the associated vectorcardiogram as shown in FIGURE 1.

Several features have been included in the simulation to approximate the normal conditions in the heart. For example, the cell located at the base of the septum is designated as the first cell to be depolarized in the simulation. In

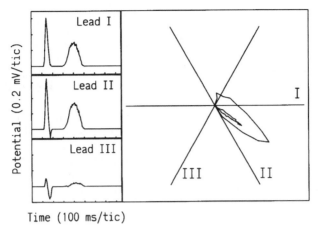

FIGURE 1. Electrocardiograms (QRS and T waves) from the three standard limb leads and the corresponding vectorcardiogram for the computer-simulated normal depolarization and repolarization of the ventricles.

addition, the greater conductivity of the His-Purkinje system is simulated by having several cells depolarize as a unit. Finally, the differences in the action potential duration of the epicardium compared to the endocardium is incorporated into the action potential algorithm of the corresponding cells.

Several abnormal conditions can be simulated with this program. Ectopic foci are simulated by designating other cells as the first to depolarize. An example of this is shown in FIGURE 2, in which a cell midway along the left

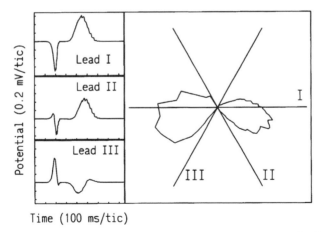

FIGURE 2. Electrocardiograms (QRS and T waves) from the three standard limb leads and the corresponding vectorcardiogram for the computer-simulated depolarization and repolarization of the ventricles with an ectopic focus located on the mid left epicardium.

epicardium was specified as the ectopic focus. Hypertrophy of one of the ventricles is simulated by increasing the magnitude of action potentials in the cells of the affected ventricle. Finally, the acute phase of a myocardial infarction can also be simulated by designating a set of cells as permanently depolarized and nonconducting. In each of these simulated abnormalities, the resulting electro- and vector-cardiograms correctly reflect the appearance of corresponding clinical observations.

The simulation is most useful if students are given the opportunity to observe the graphical representation and record the value of the potential observed by each standard limb lead given by the program at each segment of time. The students can then plot their results both as an electro- and vector-cardiogram to understand the relationship between such data and the actual events occurring in the heart. The intuition built by the exercise may then be reinforced by practice with the abnormalities that can be simulated by the computer program.

A Problem Solving Exercise That Incorporates Several Active Learning Modalities

JOSEPH BOYLE, III[a]

Associate Professor of Physiology
University of Medicine and Dentistry
New Jersey Medical School
Newark, New Jersey 07103

INTRODUCTION

Until 10–15 years ago, most science courses relied on laboratory experiences to impart a working understanding of the discipline to students. In the last 15 years the average medical physiology curriculum has suffered a 67% decline in laboratory time.[1] Some of this laboratory time has been converted into lectures. Lectures provide the faculty with an opportunity to present large volumes of information to large groups in a short time. Some faculty view this process as an *efficient* way to teach. The question that arises is: how *effective* is this method of teaching? Educators seem to be unclear as to how much learning actually occurs in the lecture setting. The amount of learning is likely to vary widely depending on the complexity of the lecture material and the organization of the lecturer. Many students must feel that the lecture is not an effective learning experience since they do not attend lectures. Many students prefer to read in the library and to study "note-service" notes which are provided from some student organization. Since most readers can read faster than people can talk this can result in a time savings.

Several years ago, the Department of Physiology at this institution initiated a problem solving approach for its conferences in the Medical Physiology Course. The aim was to provide a more active type of learning environment for the conference periods. Each of the sections of the course was assigned one problem solving session. Each of the organ system teams developed its own format for the problem solving periods. The respiratory physiology section of the course developed a combination laboratory-problem-solving format that has proven very effective. This exercise utilizes several active learning modalities which increases the effectiveness of the learning process. This same type of format is adaptable to any type of science course.

[a]Address for correspondence: Joseph Boyle, III, M.D., Department of Physiology, UMD/New Jersey Medical School, 185 South Orange Avenue, Newark, New Jersey 07103.

DESCRIPTION OF THE EDUCATIONAL ACTIVITY

The program utilizes two different curriculum periods, one as a laboratory session, the other as a symposium-discussion period. We devote two 2–hour curriculum blocks for this exercise. The first block is the laboratory period for which the class is divided into groups of 4–6 students. Three to four students in a group would be ideal, but due to class size and the number of computers, we work with groups of six students. Each group is assigned a problem. A minimum of four problems needs to be developed so that the students are exposed to several problems other than the one to which they were assigned.

In the respiratory section, each group of students is assigned a problem that they must address. TABLE 1 shows examples of some of the problems that have

TABLE 1. Examples of Assigned Problems

- Determine minute ventilation when arterial PO_2 is varied from 30 to 500 mm Hg while arterial PCO_2 is maintained between 40–45 mm Hg. Repeat measurements when $PaCO_2$ is 45–50 mm Hg and again when $PaCO_2$ is 55–60 mm Hg. Graph and interpret these results.

- Determine minute ventilation when arterial PCO_2 is varied from normal to 80 mm Hg while arterial PO_2 is 85–95 mm Hg. Repeat this procedure when airway resistance is 10 mm Hg/L/sec and again when airway resistance is 20 mm Hg/L/sec. Graph and interpret these results.

- Record changes in alveolar, arterial, and venous O_2 and CO_2 tensions when the diffusion capacity of the lung is reduced stepwise to less than 10 cc/min/mm Hg. How can the body compensate for these changes? Be able to discuss and understand the results.

- Record changes in alveolar, arterial, and venous O_2 and CO_2 tensions when the hemoglobin concentration is increased or decreased significantly. How can the body compensate for these changes? Be able to discuss and understand the results.

- Determine minute ventilation when arterial PCO_2 is varied from normal to 80 mm Hg while arterial PO_2 is 85–95 mm Hg. Repeat these recordings when arterial PO_2 is 40–50 mm Hg and again when PaO_2 is approximately 500 mm Hg. Graph and interpret these results.

- Determine the minute ventilation when arterial PO_2 is varied from 30 to 500 mm Hg while arterial PCO_2 is maintained between 40–45 mm Hg. Repeat this procedure when airway resistance is 10 mm Hg/L/sec and again when airway resistance is 20 mm Hg/L/sec. Graph and interpret these results.

- Record changes in alveolar, arterial, and venous O_2 and CO_2 tensions when the O_2 consumption is increased to 1000 mL/min. Normalize the arterial blood gases as much as possible by invoking appropriate changes in various parameters. Be able to discuss and understand the results.

- Record changes in alveolar, arterial, and venous O_2 and CO_2 tensions in response to simulated exposure to an altitude of Denver, Colorado (P_B = 625 mm Hg) and Leadville, Colorado (P_B = 523 mm Hg). Impose appropriate changes for acute and chronic exposure to these altitudes. Be able to discuss and understand the results.

been used during the past several years for the respiratory section of the course. We utilize computer simulations as a source of data for the students. These programs have been described previously.[2,3] Each group is provided with a computer during a regularly scheduled laboratory period. However, other sources of data, such as a "wet lab," previously recorded strip-chart recordings, spectral plots, graphs, tables, etc., could be utilized. Obviously, the more realistic the data collection, the closer the activity is to an actual laboratory experience. Instructors are present to lend assistance and answer questions as required. Data sheets are prepared and distributed to help in data collection. The students collect, analyze and discuss their data during the laboratory session. TABLE 2 is an example of a table of the data obtained from one of the simulation programs. The compensations shown in TABLE 2 represent physiological adjustments that a group entered after seeing the effects of a reduced barometric pressure on gas exchange.

In our schedule, the symposium-discussion period follows one week after the laboratory session. This delay is ideal since it provides time for the group to further discuss the results and prepare their data for presentation to the entire conference group. In this interval some students prepare overhead transparencies of their data or graphs which are used during the presentation. Other students use hand-drawn graphs on overhead transparencies or the chalk board to present their results. The delay also gives the group a chance to do further research into the interpretation of the data.

The conference consists of student groups that have studied four different problems. Thus, each student is exposed to three problems with which he or she is not familiar. During the symposium, a representative from each group presents the results and conclusions of the group. Following the presentation, there is an open discussion of the results. Each problem is given approximately 30 minutes of time for presentation and discussion. The student presenter serves as the moderator of the discussion, with input from the faculty member if necessary.

TABLE 2. Example of Data Table

	Simulated Altitude of Leadville, Colorado				
Intervention	P_AO_2 (mm Hg)	P_aO_2 (mm Hg)	P_aCO_2 (mm Hg)	P_vO_2 (mm Hg)	pH_a
Control (SL)	102	89	39	38	7.43
$F_IO_2 = 0.15$ ($P_B = 523$)	59	56	39	32	7.43
plus $Q_T = 7$	59	56	39	35	7.43
plus f = 18	67	64	33	37	7.48
plus Hgb = 17	67	64	33	38	7.47
plus BE = −4	67	64	33	38	7.41

ABBREVIATIONS: P_AO_2 = alveolar O_2 tension; P_aO_2 = arterial O_2 tension; P_aCO_2 = arterial CO_2 tension; P_vO_2 = venous O_2 tension; pH_a = arterial pH; SL = sea level; F_IO_2 = fraction of inspired O_2; P_B = barometric pressure; Q_T = cardiac output; f = respiratory frequency; Hgb = hemoglobin concentration (gm/dL); BE = base excess (mEq/L).

DISCUSSION

We have used this educational format within the respiratory physiology block of a medical physiology course. However, this same format could be used by any other science discipline through substitution of the appropriate laboratory experience and properly defined problems.

The problems should be selected to address major or complex points that need to be reinforced. They should be relatively well focused so that students can solve them within the allotted time. We divide our class in half because of space and equipment limitations. Eight problems are utilized to insure that students from the second half cannot copy data from the initial group. The number of problems can be varied depending on the time which is available for the symposium. However, a set of four problems for each conference was selected since this exposes each student to three problems with which he or she is not familiar. Thus, the student is exposed to new material during the conference, which makes the time spent more worthwhile.

This educational exercise was designed to use several active learning techniques to reinforce an understanding of the material. Students are exposed to a more or less real laboratory environment depending on the experimental setup that is selected. Students are involved in gathering, graphing, or tabulating data and analyzing their results. We feel that this gives them a better understanding of the data than if they were just given a graph or data to discuss. In addition, students have an opportunity to interact with their peers in a small group setting, which is known to be one of the most effective learning formats.[4] There is also a chance to interact with the faculty in a one-on-one or small group format during the laboratory. This exercise also provides the students with the opportunity to appreciate the dynamic aspects of a complex physiological system which they are unable to obtain from a textbook.

The symposium portion of this exercise is well received by the students. Our students participate in a problem-based learning (PBL) course in the first semester whereas the physiology course is in the second semester. PBL provides an opportunity for the students to present information to a small group (seven students). The problem solving format in the physiology course requires students to make presentations to a group of about 20 of their peers. This progression is generally well handled, although some students are understandably nervous in this situation. However, we feel that it is good experience and prepares them for case presentations which they will do during their clinical rotations.

There is an advantage of having a student serve as the moderator during the discussion. We have noticed that the discussion during these symposia tends to be much freer with a student in front of the group rather than a faculty member. One of our senior faculty, considered to be the best teacher in the department, has stated that this format has resulted in the best student discussion in which he has ever participated.

Overall, the students are well motivated and devote a significant effort to preparing their presentation. The physiology course has five sections and each section has a problem solving session. During the past several years we have awarded 5 to 10% of the total course grade to the student's performance during these problem solving sessions. Obviously, the grade represents a significant motivating factor. The format under discussion has only been used in the respiratory physiology block of the course. This exercise consumes a significant amount of curriculum time, i.e., four hours. The faculty that have participated in this format and many of the students have expressed the feeling that it is a worthwhile expenditure of time. We feel that it is much more effective than the typical conference run by a faculty member, which frequently deteriorates into another lecture, albeit to a small group.

SUMMARY

We have utilized a laboratory-conference exercise for several years and have found it to be an effective learning activity. The students are divided into groups of 4–6. Each group is assigned a problem or question which is designed to emphasize one or more major physiological principles. Two 2-hour periods in the curriculum are utilized for this activity. The first period is a laboratory session, staffed by faculty, where each group collects data related to its problem. The second session is a conference, ideally separated from the laboratory meeting by several days to a week. The delay allows the students time to prepare and analyze their data. The conference is a mini-symposium with a knowledgeable faculty member as an observer and an arbiter, if required. Four different groups (problems) are assigned to each conference session so that 16–24 students are present; thus, each student is exposed to three problems with which he or she is not familiar. Each group assigns a student who describes the problem, presents the data, and discusses the results. An adequate period is allowed for open discussion by the entire conference group. This problem solving exercise provides a number of educational benefits. Students have an opportunity to work with dynamic physiological relationships, interact with faculty, collect and analyze data, engage in peer group teaching, ask questions in both a laboratory and conference format, and give an oral presentation to their peers.

REFERENCES

1. BOYLE, III, J. 1985. Respsyst: An interactive microcomputer program for education. Physiologist **28:** 452–453.
2. BOYLE, III, J. 1991. A ventilatory control (Ventrol) simulation for education. Am. J. Physiol. **261** (Adv. Physiol. Ed. 6): S 25–29.
3. CARLIN, R. D. 1989. Survey results and a recommendation for a change in U.S. medical physiology curricula. Acad. Med. **64:** 202–207.
4. TOSTESON, D. C. 1986. Medical education in the computer age. In Medical Education in the Information Age: Proceedings of the Symposium on Medical Informatics: 71–78. Association of American Medical Colleges. Washington, DC.

Teaching Evolutionary Principles in the Comparative Physiology Laboratory

RONALD EDWARDS

Department of Zoology
223 Bartram Hall
University of Florida
Gainesville, Florida 32611

By definition, a comparative laboratory exercise demonstrates differences between organisms. These differences fall into separate, well-defined categories that significantly affect the meaning of the exercise; if these categories are not made clear to the students and identified for each comparison, their ability to learn both the details and the meaning of the comparison will be impaired.

There are four categories, based on cross-referencing evolutionary origin and function (FIG. 1). This concept is widely recognized as essential to learning functional details at the anatomical level. It applies equally at the physiological level. Failing to introduce and reinforce this principle has several negative consequences. The students come to believe that biology simply doesn't address functional differences between organisms and that they must learn each difference as a case to be memorized, without relation to any other. Therefore, they expend more energy per assignment and concentrate on memorization because they lack the conceptual framework for the material. They will certainly accumulate physiological details, but they will not learn about the physiology of organisms; they will not be able to predict or understand new phenomena but will simply add them to the list of things to memorize.

If the organisms being compared do the same thing in the same way and they share an ancestor that did (or does) it as well, their features are synapomorphic and there is no reason to explain the similarity in adaptive terms. In the laboratory, this is usually represented by using a certain organism as an illustration of some function understood to occur in another organism: for example, the nerves and muscles of a frog's leg can be used to demonstrate the same impulse phenomena as those of mammals.

If the animals have an organ or system shared with a common ancestor, but one has modified it for a distinct purpose and therefore demonstrates different features, the technical term is apomorphy. In this case, it is appropriate to discuss adaptive explanations for the differences. For example, the turtle's heart has two atria and one ventricle, but the mammal heart has two atria and two ventricles. They have the same origin but different functional features. The mammalian heart evolved from an ancestor with a heart very much like a turtle's; its features are an adaptation to a mammalian lifestyle.

If the animals' organs or systems do not share an ancestor with a similar or intermediate feature but are rather alike in some way, they represent a case of convergence. This difference does require an adaptive answer: evolutionary

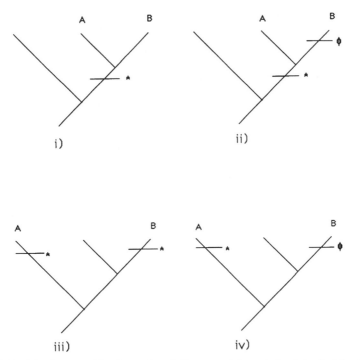

FIGURE 1. The four combinations of evolutionary origin and physiological function: i) synapomorphy, ii) apomorphy, iii) convergence, and iv) separate origin and different function.

pressures have produced, in this case, similar solutions to similar problems. For example, hemoglobin and hemocyanin represent separate, similar means to bind oxygen into blood.

Finally, if the animals' organs or systems are not shared with a common ancestor and do not resemble one another, this difference does not require an adaptive explanation; in fact, attempting to do so is the worst form of "adaptationism." The difference is simply an example of historical diversity. For example, human hemoglobin demonstrates a Bohr shift to the right with lowered pH, but horseshoe crab hemocyanin shifts to the left.

Improving one's laboratory section by emphasizing these principles does not require any changes in technique or procedure, but only in presentation and reinforcement. The laboratory manual's introduction to the procedures should explicitly identify the type of evolutionary comparison for a given exercise. Students' assignments should require them to evaluate the results of the comparison in their proper evolutionary context. This aspect of their assignment should be graded as rigorously as their tables or statistics.

The principles of homology and function would aid teaching in the laboratory regardless of whether they are taught in lecture. They would be a cost-effective addition: the students will learn everything else far more efficiently and accurately. It is not necessary to include complex information about cladistics or all the organisms on a given evolutionary tree; the models displayed here are adequate. The alternative is not attractive. I contend that physiology represents a single level of analysis of the phenomenon of animal diversity, and that the principles presented here are fundamental to understanding that diversity. Ignoring them removes the biology from physiology.

ACKNOWLEDGMENTS

I wish to thank Drs. John Anderson and David Evans of the Department of Zoology at the University of Florida for their comments and encouragement.

Active Learning in Cardiovascular Physiology

H. H. ERICKSON[a] AND V. L. CLEGG[b]

[a]Department of Anatomy and Physiology
College of Veterinary Medicine; and
[b]Office of Educational Advancement
Kansas State University
Manhattan, Kansas 66506-5602

We are initiating active problem-based learning in the classroom and laboratories in the College of Veterinary Medicine at Kansas State University. Faculty are using both large and small group problem-based learning methods. Both strategies require students to take more responsibility for their learning, to actively work toward understanding specific problems, and to teach one another through student interaction. Bonwell and Eison,[1] recently reported that research has clearly demonstrated that the more college students become involved with the education process, the more they learn.

In the teaching of cardiovascular physiology, active learning laboratories consist of a demonstration of heart valve function in the equine heart; participation laboratories where students record and analyze their own electrocardiograms (ECGs) and the ECGs of a dog and pony; two computer-based programs on the physiology of the heart and arrhythmias; and a heart sounds teaching system.

A new computer laboratory has been developed which consists of 35 IBM compatible 386 MHz computers networked to Novell file servers. Two software programs (from Cardionics, Houston) have been used in the computer laboratory. The first program, a basic cardiac teaching system, teaches blood flow through the heart, electrical flow within the heart, ECG lead systems, basic measurements, and waveforms. The second program (TABLE 1) is a tutorial in

TABLE 1. Arrhythmia Teaching System

1. Normal sinus	14. Junctional tachycardia
2. Sinus bradycardia	15. Supraventricular tachycardia
3. Sinus tachycardia	16. AV dissociation
4. Sinus arrhythmia	17. 1st Degree AV block
5. Wandering pacemaker	18. 2nd Degree AV block (Mobitz Type I)
6. Sinus arrest (block)	19. 2nd Degree AV block (Mobitz Type II)
7. Premature atrial contractions	20. 3rd Degree AV block (complete block)
8. Atrial tachycardia	21. Premature ventricular contraction
9. Atrial flutter	22. Idioventricular rhythm(s)
10. Atrial fibrillation	23. Ventricular tachycardia
11. Premature junctional contractions	24. Ventricular fibrillation
12. Junctional escape	25. Asystole
13. Accelerated junctional rhythm	26. Pacemaker-AV sequential

TABLE 2. Student Evaluation of Learning Methods

Learning Method	Score
Basic Cardiac Teaching System in computer lab	4.35
Arrhythmia Teaching System in computer lab	4.34
Laboratory experiment to record ECG of dog	4.27
Laboratory experiment to record their own ECG	4.01
Syllabus on cardiovascular physiology	3.86
Video tape: Heart Sounds and Murmurs	3.49
Video tape: Life Under Pressure	3.49
Heart sounds teaching system	3.38
Video tape: Cardiac Cycle of the Dog	3.28
Video tape: Two Hearts that Beat as One	3.24
Bolton's *Handbook of Canine and Feline Electrocardiography*	3.09
Lab experiment: ECG and Heart Sounds of the Pony	3.00
Human Physiology (by Schauf, Moffett, and Moffett)	2.35
Library Research Project	2.22

NOTE: This evaluation (by 82 students) rated active learning methods best. Scoring is from very low (1) to very high (5).

ECG interpretation, consisting of 26 basic arrhythmias. It has several modes of operation: a demonstration mode that presents live wave forms and explanatory text, a comparison mode, and a quiz mode.

Our experience is that computer-based learning increases the opportunities for active learning, uses fewer faculty and graduate student teaching assistants in the laboratories, decreases the use of live animals, and improves student skills in problem solving and information handling. In a survey of 82 students, active learning experiences received the highest rating, with the computer laboratories receiving the highest scores (TABLE 2).

REFERENCE

1. BONWELL, C. C. & J. A. EISON, Eds. 1991. Active Learning: Creating Excitement in the Classroom. ASHE-ERIC Higher Education Report No. 1. The George Washington University, School of Education and Human Development. Washington, D.C.

Promoting Active Learning in Developmental Biology Using the Japanese Medaka (*Oryzias latipes*) as an Experimental Model

VICTORIA HENSON-APOLLONIO AND
ROBIN SCRIBAILO
Biological Sciences and Chemistry Section
Purdue University–North Central
Westville, Indiana 46391

INTRODUCTION

Our institution is a small regional campus located in Northwestern Indiana. Many of our students fall into nontraditional categories and the quality of preparation for college-level studies is quite variable. Students in non-science degree programs, such as Elementary Education majors, are often unsure of their ability to do well in biology courses. We have found that the inclusion of a unit utilizing a study of development in the Japanese medaka (*Oryzias latipes*) is an excellent way to promote active learning and encourage critical thinking skills while covering a complex biological topic.

The objectives of this unit include: (1) stimulation of interest in biology, especially in students that are non-science majors; (2) teaching developmental biology in a participatory manner that will inspire wonder at the remarkable processes involved; (3) introduction to concepts of critical thinking and experimental design—including making decisions on suitable quantitative and qualitative parameters and measurement; (4) methods of organization and presentation of data; (5) methods of library research to obtain information that will allow an assessment of the significance of experimental results; (6) fostering of cooperation among students by carrying out units as a small group activity; (7) encouraging the development of positive self-esteem, since experiments are interesting and most often "successful"; and (8) imbuing students with a greater appreciation and understanding of biology, so that as informed citizens they can better evaluate scientific information in the popular media.

MATERIALS AND EXPERIMENTAL DESIGN

Fish and Fish Eggs

Breeding-age Japanese medaka (*Oryzias latipes*) (4-month-old males and females) were obtained from Carolina Biological Supply Company and were propagated according to instructions in the accompanying brochure.[1] Fish were stocked in fresh water at 20 fish/20-gallon aquarium, with a ratio of 4 females: 1 male. Fish were fed twice a day with Tetramin (Tetrawerk). Water temperature was maintained at 22–27°C, and tanks were placed in a room with artificial lighting on a 16-hour light/8-hour dark cycle. Eggs were collected from females or from the aquarium tank bottom 1½–4 hours after "daylight." In order to obtain sufficient numbers of eggs at synchronized stages of development for student experiments, eggs, at blastula stage, were held at 40°C in embryo-rearing medium[1] until experiments were initiated.

Video and Still Photography

Video recordings of developing medaka embryos were made with a Panasonic Digital 5100 camera and Fuji SVHS film, #H4713. The camera was connected to a video recorder (Panasonic Corp.) or directly to the CPU (Quadra 950, Apple Corp.) utilizing VideoSpigot (SuperMac Technology). Still photographic images (FIGS. 1 and 2) were made with a Nikon FX-35DX camera and Ektachrome 100HC color slide film. Both cameras were mounted on a Nikon SMZ-U stereomicroscope. An Olympus MO21 inverted microscope was used for higher-magnification photographs. For the majority of the photographic

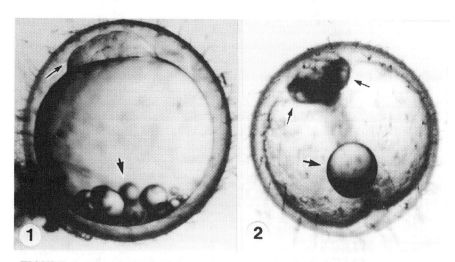

FIGURE 1. Embryo is in cleavage stage 9 (approximately 64-cell stage). Note the developing embryo (*small arrow*). *Large arrow* indicates oil droplets, directly opposite developing embryo. This stage occurs at approximately 4 hours post fertilization at 28°C.

FIGURE 2. Embryo has developed to stage 23 (46 hours at 28°C). Note that oil droplets have coalesced to form one droplet (*large arrow*). *Small arrows* indicate optic areas. Note pigmentation of retinal area and lens development.

work, embryos were held in rearing medium, although occasionally eggs were embedded in 0.2% agarose, w/v, in rearing medium.

Interactive Computer Program

Compressed video recordings and animations were incorporated into a multimedia presentation using the software Macromind Director V3.1 (Super-Mac Corp.). The presentation software, Adobe Premier and Adobe Photoshop (Adobe Corp.), were used to create special effects.

RESULTS AND DISCUSSION

In the initial introductory laboratory exercise of viewing the interactive video presentation and examining living embryos, students successfully identified and drew several stages of medaka development. The two following laboratory sessions was devoted to formulating hypotheses regarding the effect of various treatments on the development of medaka embryos. Examples of variables and agents that were tested included: salinity, temperature effects, hormones (e.g., cortisol), light levels, vitamin A, detergents, oil, O_2 levels, insecticide treatment, and water from Lake Michigan near a point source of possible pollution. Students carried out these experiments over the developmental period from blastula to hatching (or death of the embryo). Groups of 3–4 students then chose a hypothesis and designed a series of experiments to collect data to test the validity of the hypothesis. During the early stages of the experiments, a laboratory period was dedicated to teaching students how data should be reported, for both written and oral presentations. Effective methods of graphic data presentation were emphasized. In the last two laboratory periods of the medaka unit, students gave oral group presentations of their experiments.

CONCLUSIONS

On the basis of observations of student behavior and both written and informal responses of the students, the use of medaka as a model system to study vertebrate developmental biology was highly successful. Initial hostility to biology was overcome to the extent that interest level was high, as reflected by class participation and student evaluations of the courses. Students began to develop an awareness of "how science is done" and an understanding of the role of critical thinking in science, as evidenced by the unit reports. In this laboratory setting, students worked cooperatively in groups and shared the responsibility of setting up experiments and making observations. Students seemed to gain an interest and critical ability in evaluation of additional materials and scientific information gathered from the popular media. The organism itself (the medaka), instructor input, and slide and video materials stimulated the interest of the students. Inclusion of video material also provided a "friendly" method for computer usage in the classroom that greatly enhanced the learning experience. Because of their increased enthusiasm for biology, many students felt more positive that as elementary school instructors they would now want to teach biology, particularly in a "hands on" approach. In general, students seemed to feel that after this series of laboratories they would be better able to evaluate and understand reports of biological information.

SUMMARY

We use the Japanese medaka (*Oryzias latipes*) as an animal model for developmental studies in our introductory biology courses. These courses are designed for Elementary Education majors and students in non-science degree programs. Introduction to the topic involves observation of live medaka embryos at various stages of development. These observations are guided by video clips and still photographs, which have been incorporated into an interactive computer presentation. In subsequent labs, students perform experiments that they have designed, which utilize medaka embryos. Most choose to test the effect of various environmental treatments on normal development. We plan to end this unit with a "medaka symposium" in which the students will present data from their own experiments in posters or talks. We hope to reinforce students' confidence in their ability to perform and understand scientific investigation. Students have been very favorable in their evaluation of the medaka unit as a learning tool.

ACKNOWLEDGMENTS

We express appreciation for technical assistance and advice from William Henson, Mark Walker, Dr. Shihong Chen, Purdue University-North Central; and Dr. Clark Gedney, Dr. Christopher A. Bidwell, Dr. Kent Blacklidge, Purdue University-West Lafayette.

REFERENCE

1. KIRCHEN, R. V. & W. R. WEST. The Japanese Medaka: Its Care and Development. Carolina Biological Supply Company. Burlington, NC.

For Teaching Physiology, a Partially Integrated Medical Curriculum Is Not a Bad Arrangement

JOHN N. HOWELL

Department of Biological Sciences
Ohio University College of Osteopathic Medicine (OUCOM)
Athens, Ohio 45701

Students here at OUCOM have scored particularly well in physiology on the National Boards (Osteopathic) Part I, but not in other disciplines. Anecdotal reports from clinical faculty and feedback from students are consistent with the idea that our students' knowledge of physiology is relatively strong. In this paper the reasons for this are examined.

OUCOM Board scores in physiology between 1985 and 1992 averaged 8.6% above the national means, while scores in other disciplines hovered around the national means, anatomy averaging 2.5% above and others below (FIG. 1). Between 1978, the first year in which OUCOM students took boards, and 1984, scores were not provided. However, the percent failure rate told the same story. Fewer failures occurred in physiology than in other disciplines.

At OUCOM, physiology has been taught during both of the first two years of the medical curriculum (TABLE 1). During the first year, cellular processes (membrane transport, excitability and contractility) are emphasized (23 hours over 4.5 weeks) and introductions to the cardiovascular, respiratory, renal and

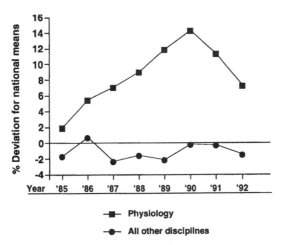

FIGURE 1. National Osteopathic Board Scores at OUCOM from 1985 through 1992.

TABLE 1. Ohio University College of Osteopathic Medicine Curriculum Summary, Years I and II (1992)

	Contact Hours		
	Total[a]	Lab	Physiology component[b]
Fall Quarter, Year I—10 weeks			
Gross Anatomy I	101	71	
Microanatomy	51	28	
Medical Biochemistry I	28		
Osteopathic Clinical Practice I	54	26	
Winter Quarter, Year I—10 weeks			
Infection & Immunity I	46	14	
Gross Anatomy II	107	80	
Medical Physiology	47		47
Medical Biochemistry II	22		
Osteopathic Clinical Practice II	62	35	
Spring Quarter, Year I—10 weeks			
Infection & Immunity II	51	18	
Endocrinology & Metabolism I	29		11
Pharmacology	46		
Pathology & Laboratory Medicine	69	18	
Osteopathic Clinical Practice III	64	31	
Fall Quarter, Year II—10 weeks			
Neural System	108		10
Musculoskeletal System	56		11
Osteopathic Clinical Practice IV	90	34	
Winter Quarter, Year II—10 weeks			
Cardiovascular System	104	6	32
Respiratory System	71	2	19
Osteopathic Clinical Practice V	87	48	
Spring Quarter, Year II—9 weeks			
Gastrointestinal System	78		6
Urogenital System	37		8
Endocrinology & Metabolism II	37		7
Gynecology	26		
Osteopathic Clinical Practice VI	63	20	

[a]Total hours includes lectures, demonstration and labs, but not examinations.
[b]The physiology component is identified primarily as hours taught by physiologists. A few hours not taught by physiologists are also specified as physiology.

endocrine systems follow (35 hours). During the second year, significant physiology components are incorporated into each of seven systems courses, totaling 93 contact hours, giving a grand total of 151 hours spread over two years. All but 23 hours are conventional lecture presentations. The others are: 6 hours of laboratory work, 2 hours of demonstrations, 4 hours of problem-set discussions, 1 hour of case study discussion, and 10 hours of discussions of assigned papers in the literature. The OUCOM total is significantly above the national average of 100.1 lecture hours of physiology.[1] The teaching is done primarily by five Ph.D. physiologists who teach both in the first and second years. None of the five have participated in setting the Board exams and no attempt is made to teach to the Boards. Use is made of supplemental computer learning packages and audiovisuals in some areas. Course exams are mostly multiple-choice questions with a small, but significant, fraction of essay and short-answer questions. Because not all of the students pass the introductory physiology course the first time, the course is also offered in the summer on a remediation basis.

Two factors probably account for the high Board scores in physiology. First is the number of hours devoted to physiology. Second, and probably more important, is that the teaching is spread over five quarters, with well over half of it coming in the second year, at the end of which students take the Board exams. Although the stress level is very high during the introductory course in the first year, when students are taking four other courses as well, the OUCOM physiology curriculum appears to be effective. At present there is little inclination among the physiologists here toward major restructuring.

REFERENCE

1. CARLIN, R. D. 1989. Survey results and a recommendation for a change in U.S. medical physiology curricula. Acad. Med. **64:** 202–207.

Teaching Renal Physiology Concepts Using a Problem Solving Approach

HERBERT F. JANSSEN

Departments of Orthopaedic Surgery and Physiology
Texas Tech University Health Sciences Center
Lubbock, Texas 79430

Mastering the concepts involved in renal physiology is a challenge for students and presenting them effectively is, similarly, a challenge for professors. Understanding these concepts and their practical application requires a higher level of thought processing than is required for reciting simple facts. Frequently, textbooks approach this topic using the same rote memory approach that is applied to other areas. Students who are taught renal physiology using a rote memory approach may be successful at calculating simple renal clearance values; however, they often appear to lack the insight needed to logically apply this concept in evaluating the excretion of unfamiliar compounds.

Creating a setting that encourages learning conceptual material at an analysis level can be difficult. Classroom and clinic time constraints can inhibit the desired level of concentration required to master these problems. A teaching tool used at our institution has been found effective in reducing this frustration. A programmed-learning text provides students with the opportunity to develop and test their ability to analyze and evaluate new situations related to the renal processing of different compounds. Problems are presented that require the student to calculate flow rate and solute movement at various points along a stylized nephron. In most situations, requested values can be calculated mentally, thus reducing the emphasis on mathematics and allowing the student to concentrate on the concept being applied. Each example or problem is followed by the solution and a written explanation of how the solution is derived. The data provided in subsequent examples are changed. This requires the student to approach each problem in a logical, problem solving manner rather than simply using a memorized approach.

FIGURE 1 shows a page from the problem solving text that presents the solution to the first problem the students are asked to solve regarding inulin excretion. The page immediately preceding this solution would include only the numbers shown in the shaded areas. In addition to these values, the students are given a G-T balance value. Based upon this information, the students are asked to provide the remaining answers. This solution to the problem is followed by a written description of how the answers can be obtained. In addition to the inulin example, the students are asked to solve problems that involve a compound that is secreted by the renal tubules (*p*-aminohippuric acid) and a compound that is reabsorbed (glucose). In these examples, concentrations are selected that require the student to evaluate conditions that involve transport maximum.

FIGURE 2 illustrates the solution to the first problem covered in the urinary

116

Inulin Example 1

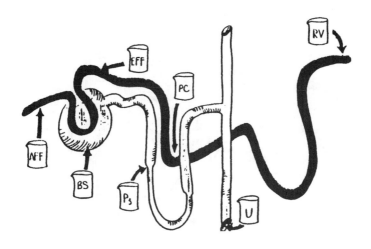

site	Amount/min (mg/min)	Flow Rate (ml/min)	Concentration (mg/ml)	TF/P ratio
AFF	500	500	1	
BS	100	100	1	1
EFF	400	400	1	
P3	100	33	3	3
PC	400	467		
RV	400	499	0.8	
U	100	1	100	100

FIGURE 1. The solution to an example problem on inulin excretion.

concentrating mechanisms chapter. As in the previous example, the numbers in the shaded area are provided and the students are asked to calculate the remaining values. Once again, this solution is followed by a written description of how the answers can be derived.

An additional chapter addresses issues involved in body fluid balance. The examples include changes in water and sodium levels that alter fluid distribution between intracellular and extracellular spaces. The final chapter reviews inconsistencies that exist in the equations that are normally used to calculate renal

Urine Concentration Example 1 – normal ADH

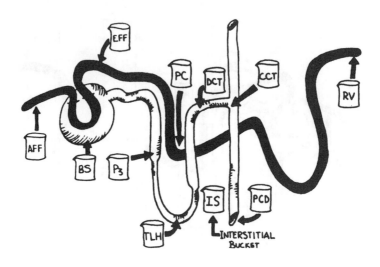

Site	Fluid Concentration mOsm/kg H$_2$O	Flow Rate (ml / min)	Inulin Concentration (mg / ml)	Inulin TF/p ratio
AFF	300	500	1	
BS	300	100	1	1
EFF	302	400	1	
P3	300	33	3	3
PC	300	467		
TLH	600	16.5	6.25	6.25
DCT	150	16.5	6.25	6.25
CCT	300	4.5	12.0	12.0
PCD	600	1.5	66.7	66.7
IS	600			
RV	299	498.5	0.80	

FIGURE 2. The solution to an example problem on urinary concentrating mechanisms.

clearance, renal plasma flow, and the renal extraction ratio. The discussion of these problems includes a review of why they exist and how they affect the calculated values.

Our experience with this approach has proven successful at providing students with an opportunity to develop their skills at understanding conceptual material. It is felt that this approach can also be used successfully in a computer-based learning format. Currently, plans are under way to accomplish this goal.

Improved Student Performance Following the Introduction of Socratic Teaching Methods for Basic Science Courses in Pharmacy School

JAMES L. JUNKER, GEORGE A. W. WATERHOUSE,
AND ROBERT L. GARRETT

Department of Pharmaceutical Sciences
Campbell University School of Pharmacy
Buies Creek, North Carolina 27506

INTRODUCTION

Socratic teaching techniques are widely used in higher education, most notably in law. However, they are generally not a part of basic science instruction. In order to test these techniques in a biomedical context, a Socratic style of teaching has been introduced into three courses, Pharmacology III, Pathology, and Human Anatomy and Physiology II, which make up 14% of the didactic curriculum of a four-year, entry-level Pharm.D. program. Class size averages 65. The interactive or "Socratic" aspect of the method is that instead of listening to lectures, students are randomly selected to answer questions related to that day's material. To varying degrees, student answers are amplified by the instructors to ensure adequate understanding of basic concepts by the class. Students are given lecture handouts, which they are expected to study prior to the class period. Textbook reading is required in Anatomy/Physiology and Pathology. Further incentive for keeping up with assigned material is provided by weekly unannounced quizzes.

RESULTS

Course grades, based on scores in exams and quizzes, are used to evaluate student performance (FIG. 1). When "Socratic" classes were compared to "pre-Socratic" classes, Pharmacology and Pathology classes showed significant improvement. The apparent improvement in the one Anatomy/Physiology class was not statistically significant.

DISCUSSION

The typical pattern, in which students sit and write lecture notes for multiple class periods and then cram intensely the day or two before an examination, is

120

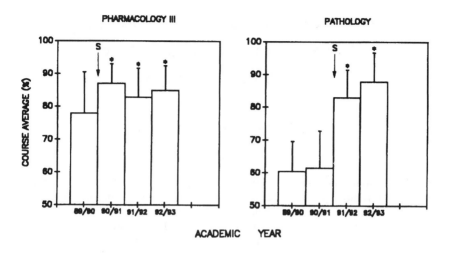

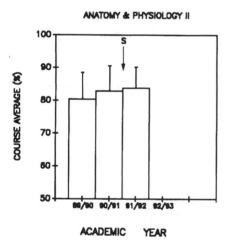

FIGURE 1. Histograms showing course averages for Pharmacology III, Pathology, and Anatomy/Physiology. *Arrows* indicate when the Socratic method was introduced. *Error bars* indicate standard deviation. An asterisk indicates a significant improvement ($p < 0.01$) in class average compared to the pre-Socratic average.

interrupted by the Socratic method described here. The daily possibility of a quiz and of being called upon in class provide incentive for the students to study daily. Since the students keep up with the material, studying for exams is more a matter of consolidation of materials already studied than of cramming in new material. Therefore, the Socratic method has shown best results in Pharmacology and Pathology, courses where the amount of information is the greatest.

Plans are to continue the method (even in Anatomy/Physiology) because, in addition to what can be measured in course averages, the Socratic method encourages students to be more responsible for their own learning, to learn from reading, and to explain orally to others what they have learned. Thus, students are better equipped to become independent learners and scientific communicators, skills which have lifelong value.

Problem Solving in Neurobiology Using Clinical Case Studies in Small Groups

ROBERT A. LAVINE

The George Washington University
School of Medicine and Health Sciences
Washington, DC 20037

Active learning and problem solving were promoted in an interdisciplinary clinical neurobiology course (combining neurophysiology and neuroanatomy) by discussing clinical case studies in small groups. Each case followed lectures and laboratory sessions on a particular level of the nervous system, i.e., peripheral nerve and spinal cord, brain stem, and cerebrum. Summaries of case-history and physical findings were distributed before each group session, and discussions were facilitated by faculty or residents using recommended questions. Written case reports were required. Several issues of administration and assessment were addressed. Student feedback over two years suggests that this method increased knowledge and stimulated learning.

As an example of a case study, after attending lectures on somatic sensation and spinal cord, students were given a written history of a man who noted a loss of pain and temperature sensation in the left foot and calf three years prior to admission and weakness of the right arm two years prior to admission, and who now complains that he has difficulty walking. The examination revealed an absence of pain and temperature sensation on the left side of the body below the mid-cervical level and a generalized diminution of position and vibratory sensation in all four extremities.

The group leaders were asked to moderate a one-hour discussion based on a series of discussion questions. Students were asked to provide a problem list, discuss alternative bases for these problems, and localize the lesion (in this case,

TABLE 1. Student Evaluation of Effects of Presentation on Learning[a]

Course Component	Evaluation on Scale of 1 through 5[b]				
	1	2	3	4	5
Case studies	24	42	24	10	1
Basic lectures	6	31	46	15	1
Anatomy text	23	30	23	16	7
Physiology text	24	30	34	9	3
Anatomy atlas	6	19	25	27	22
Laboratory sessions	4	17	40	28	11

[a]Evaluation scale: 1 = stimulated learning, 5 = interfered with learning.
[b]Table items are percentages of respondents.

TABLE 2. Student Evaluation of Effects of Presentation on Learning[a]

Course Component	Mean	Standard Deviation
Case studies	2.24	0.97
Basic lectures	2.76	0.84
Anatomy text	2.54	1.22
Physiology text	2.31	1.09
Anatomy atlas	3.40	1.21
Laboratory sessions	3.25	1.00

NOTE: n ranged from 63 to 72; data are presented for 1992 course.
[a]Evaluation scale: 1 = stimulated learning, 5 = interfered with learning.

a tumor in the right lateral funiculus of the cervical spinal cord above C5 that enlarged to involve both posterior columns). After trying various formats, we now assess students' learning by means of one-page typed reports, graded on a Pass-Fail basis, and by multiple-choice questions, based upon the case studies, that are included in the written examination.

Ten group leaders were recruited each year, allowing the class to be divided into groups of about 17 students each. Group leaders have been neurology faculty and residents, and basic science faculty, but the latter concluded that clinical experience was important in facilitating group discussion. The clinical leaders have reacted favorably and most volunteered to continue leading these groups in successive years.

Student feedback on a 5-point scale (TABLES 1 and 2) were 1 = stimulated learning, 5 = interfered with learning, most recently rated the presentation of case studies (M = 2.24, SD = 0.97) as quite helpful in comparison to other course components. These results show that even limited time devoted to small group problem solving can contribute to neurobiology education.

A Method of Improving Student Learning in Physiology: A Pilot Experiment

CHARLES J. McKINLEY AND WILLIAM R. STOLL

Biology Department
Albany College of Pharmacy
Albany, New York 12208

This is a preliminary report on our efforts to transform standard physiology laboratory exercises into "workshops," and no longer involve all that is attendant in that approach. Our prime concern in this experiment was to focus on encouraging students' involvement in our course. If successful, this would increase their comprehension and recall of topic material beyond the previous routine, which included laboratories. While we have used many of the body systems from standard labs, we have altered them in various ways to eliminate "cookbook" procedures and complex equipment. Typically, the workshop exercises will depict physiological data, graphs, tables, and leading questions. In our new approach, students are responsible for understanding principles, providing predictions of outcomes, understanding significance of data, interpreting information, and locating factual material.

In our pilot approach, students are required to engage in a new workshop on alternate weeks of class. All receive a copy of the current workshop in advance of their scheduled appearance at the workshop. During this interval, many will have completed a part of the exercise by using their text and the reference, which is on reserve in the learning center. At the workshop, students are randomly distributed in groups of 5–6, where the groups work together for approximately 2 hours, to complete their exercises, using the text and reference.

Supported by the instructor, who serves as facilitator, the groups are encouraged and directed in their efforts to obtain necessary information. These groups are responsible for exchange of ideas among their members, and final answers and solutions for the various problems become a group effort in this approach; each group delegates work assignments among themselves. They share and discuss information and insights they have gained in working on each question and problem. After all groups have finished the given workshop, an assessment includes a 20-question quiz over the content.

Early results are subjective; however, it appears that improvements include test scores on workshop topics, indicating overall better grades in the course. In working with the students throughout the semester, there is a positive feeling that course concepts and essentials are more thoroughly learned. Concepts are more readily recalled, as needed, in pharmacology and related courses in the following year. Students also appear more willing and able to use scientific terms in explaining functions and interactions in the body. At least as important, the course evaluation shows that many students liked the workshop approach.

Our prediction is that this approach would work in any science course for most health care professionals.

The authors would be most happy to provide more details, or examples of our effort, to any faculty interested in this low-tech approach, explaining further benefits which might be appealing to other instructors. Contact the senior author at Albany College of Pharmacy, Biology Department, 106 New Scotland Ave., Albany, New York 12208. FAX (518) 445-7202; Phone (518) 445-7269.

Use of Simulation Software in an Advanced Physiology Research Course

EDWARD P. MEYERTHOLEN

Department of Physiology and Health Science
Ball State University
Muncie, Indiana 47306

My department has recently revised the research course that is required of advanced undergraduate and masters degree students. This course is designed to introduce the student to the basic principles of scientific research and to acquaint the student with the application of various laboratory procedures used in physiological research. The course format consists of a series of research/technical projects to be completed by the students. These projects include a variety of techniques from classical physiology as well as more modern techniques from cell and molecular biology. In addition to the variety of "wet labs," computer simulation software is used to attempt to introduce the students to the basics of experimental design, data analysis, and data presentation.

This course employs the integrated human physiology software HUMAN developed by T. Coleman (University of Mississippi Medical Center) and J. Randall (Indiana University). This software models the major physiological systems (body fluids, heart, kidneys, the peripheral circulation, respiratory system, acid-base balance, etc.), allowing the student to vary up to 67 different physiological parameters and follow the response of over 100 different computed variables. In this course, the software is used to allow students to become more fully acquainted with the mechanics of research, especially with regard to data presentation.

Students are required to select a specific research project, design an experimental protocol, and complete the project using data collected from the simulation. A completed project will include a "simulated" paper, an oral presentation of their results, and the preparation of a grant proposal for follow-up research.

The paper required of the students is expected to be a manuscript prepared as if for publication. The students are therefore expected to prepare a background literature review for their project; they must determine what techniques would have been used to perform their project, collect and analyze their data, and finally prepare their data for the manuscript. They must therefore acquire strategies for effective literature searches as well as understand the basics of data analysis and presentation to complete this aspect of the project. Finally, they must organize their material so as to present their information clearly and logically to their audience.

The requirement of an oral presentation of their results and conclusions is an attempt to expose the students to one of the primary methods used in science to convey new information. The presentations are part of a minisymposium in which all students in the class must prepare a 10–12 minute talk (with time for questions) in which they are required to present their experiments and conclusions. This allows the student the opportunity to learn how to give an effective oral presentation.

Finally, students are required to prepare a grant proposal in which they are to propose a continuation of their research project: in this way, they will reexamine the results of their projects and understand that all questions have not been answered.

I feel that this use of computer simulation allows the student to be exposed to an important aspect of scientific research that is often neglected in undergraduate education, that of communication. In addition, while the ideal situation would be for each student to perform "real" research in the laboratory, this is impractical in many universities because of limitations of space and money. This is an alternative approach that we use in conjunction with other projects; its aim is to expose students to a research environment so that they may better understand fundamental principles of experimental design, strategies and protocols for effective literature searches, analysis and presentation of data, and critical analysis of journal articles.

Using Computer-Aided Instruction (CAI) to Promote Active Learning in the Physiology Classroom

T. M. NOSEK,[a] G. C. BOND, J. M. GINSBURG,
R. E. GODT, W. F. HOFMAN, W. J. JACKSON,
T. F. OGLE, S. P. PORTERFIELD, S. D. STONEY, Jr.,
V. T. WIEDMEIER, J. A. WORK, L. A. LEWIS,
AND M. LEVY

CAI Research and Development Group
Department of Physiology and Endocrinology
Medical College of Georgia
Augusta, Georgia 30912-3000

Teaching faculties face numerous problems preparing students for careers in the life and medical sciences. The approximate doubling of scientific knowledge every 5.5 years, coupled with the mandate to educate students from diverse educational and cultural backgrounds in a financial environment that dictates large class sizes with little opportunity for personalized instruction, indicates the need for new academic strategies.

The use of computer-aided instruction (CAI) in the health sciences dates from the late 1960s and early 1970s.[1] A recent critical review of the use of CAI in the health professions conducted by Cohen and Dacanay[2] concludes that CAI contributes to the effectiveness of teaching. Beneficial qualities include active involvement of the students even when the class size is large, directive feedback, and realistic stimuli. Studies have shown that CAI can decrease the time needed by faculty to present information[3] and the time required by students to master the information.[4] Unfortunately, relatively few CAI applications presently exist in the health sciences. This deficiency represents the greatest obstacle to achieving the desired educational impact of CAI.

In response to these issues, and given the availability of relatively inexpensive hardware and hypertext development software, a faculty member at the Medical College of Georgia developed a CAI application (using Linkway by IBM) in the area of membrane transport and electrophysiology in the Medical Physiology course taught to 200 first year medical and graduate students. It consisted of a set of objectives, a brief outline of the lectures, and a set of hypermedia multiple-choice questions (adaptive testing format) keyed to the outline. Student evaluation by the Class of 1995 with a Likert-scaled questionnaire indicated that over 82% of the class used the application (4.2 hours on average), found it a worthwhile learning resource, recommended its use by other

[a]Address for correspondence: Thomas M. Nosek, Ph.D., Coordinator, CAI R&D Group, Department of Physiology & Endocrinology, Medical College of Georgia, Augusta, Georgia 30912-3000.

students, and encouraged further development of CAI. Perceived benefits included: (1) attention keeping, (2) concise review, (3) identification of problem areas, (4) provision of immediate feedback and detailed explanations, and (5) self-paced learning. It is the general consensus of the faculty and students that this application has increased the quality of our learning environment. We learned that for a CAI application to be utilized, it must: (1) put the student in control of the learning resource, (2) minimize hardware requirements so as not to intimidate the students, (3) present high quality text and illustrative material, (4) be fully integrated into the course, (5) be formally introduced to the student, and (6) have its content tested over.

With the support of our dean and chairman, 14 faculty members formed a CAI Research and Development Group to create a multimedia Windows 3.1 application (using ToolBook by Asymetrix) which encompasses all areas of Physiology. This project is presently in progress and is based on the sound educational principles of readiness, advance organizers (objectives), reinforcement, involvement, and evaluation. In addition to the format of the prototype, this fully indexed application will contain detailed text enhanced with graphics, animation, and interactive digital video (DVI) to explain and reinforce each point of the course outline. Appropriate questions test for mastery of important concepts or facts. The program response is tailored to the student's answer selection (adaptive testing). Correct answers are acknowledged and the underlying physical principle explained. The response to an incorrect answer includes additional information and the opportunities to either answer the original question again or apply the principle to a different question. Clinical problems and case studies are also included to emphasize and encourage problem solving.

As the application is integrated into the course, we anticipate that it will enable us to: (1) decrease the number of large group lectures where faculty time is spent primarily in didactic activities; (2) enhance student-faculty interaction in more informal, small group, question-and-answer sessions; (3) provide a more pleasant, active learning environment; (4) enhance problem solving and independent learning skills; and (5) increase the efficiency of learning.

REFERENCES

1. PIEMME, T. E. 1988. Computer-assisted learning and evaluation in medicine. JAMA **260:** 367–372.
2. COHEN, P. A. & L. S. DACANAY. 1992. Computer-based instruction and health professions education. Eval. Health Prof. **15:** 259–281.
3. TEYLER, T. J. & T. J. VONEIDA. 1992. Use of computer-assisted courseware in teaching neuroscience: the Graphic Brain. Am. J. Physiol. Adv. Physiol. Ed. **263:** S37–S44.
4. MARION, R., B. R. NIEBUHR, E. R. PETRUSA, *et al.* 1982. Computer-based instruction in basic medical science education. J. Med. Ed. **57:** 521–526.

Promoting Active Learning in a Large Introductory Biology Course through Writing[a]

ROGER PERSELL

Department of Biological Sciences
Hunter College
New York, New York 10021

Principles of Biology at Hunter College is typical of many large introductory college science courses. Constructed around a customary survey of topics found in most encyclopedic biology textbooks, the course serves nearly 700 non-resident students each semester, the majority of whom are women and minority students from the New York City area. Students rely on graduate teaching assistants, often non-native English speakers, to direct laboratory and recitation/discussion sections. Comparably to many other large science courses, Principles of Biology suffers from high attrition, meager enthusiasm, and frustration over the unworkable tradition of "covering" an ever-expanding body of knowledge. An emphasis on "transmitting facts" from lecturer to student and on recall testing heightens an atmosphere of anxiety over memorizing every word, diagram and abstract concept. Even the course's dedicated computer learning center—the Socrates Center—has provided little more than drilling in multiple-choice examinations.

To address these curricular problems, we have begun the first of a two-year model program with five related objects: (1) To increase active student participation in learning through the wide use of informal, nongraded writing projects in recitation and lecture sections, in the Socrates Center, and in the laboratory. Under the guidance of teaching assistants, students construct sample exam questions, summaries of text pages, and concept definitions. The rubric for these activities is "writing-to-learn,"[1] but students also formulate their own understanding of ideas in biology by sketching, diagramming, and graphing. Peer exchange and evaluation of nongraded writing lead to the construction of concepts in the students' own language which can then be measured confidently against the language of the text or instructor. (2) To upgrade the course's computer facility for wordprocessing and networked conversational software. (3) To relate biology to relevant social and political issues through specific reading/discussion/writing assignments. (4) To train graduate teaching assistants to lead discussions and organize collaborative projects. (5) To employ advanced undergraduates who have benefited from these innovations as peer tutors and leaders of computer-assisted collaborative writing and learning.

Results from the first semester of this project are based on four experimental recitation sections out of a total of fourteen. The two graduate assistants as-

[a]This project has been supported in part by NSF Curriculum Development Grant USE-9155893.

130

signed to the sections have been using teaching styles formulated primarily by the Institute for Writing and Thinking at Bard College (Annandale-on-Hudson, New York). The first phase of a Macintosh-platform Local Area Network (LAN) has recently been installed in the Socrates Center. The earliest evidence is based on interviews and student evaluations, although pre- and post-testing is being analyzed for both control and experimental sections.

Students initially offered considerable resistance and objections to anything different from the traditional dichotomies of lecture/note-taking and question/answering. Some requested a change in section. For those who stayed, reports emphasized "surprise" at how much easier the course seemed than expected, in contrast to students from control groups. Standard Hunter College student evaluations of teaching assistants led to the highest marks for one of the experimental instructors; her marks were also the highest she has received. Students reported a sense of acquiring new skill at studying, not just new biology vocabulary. A surprise occurred when students began to compare teaching innovations in biology with their other science courses; they reported complaining about the rigid format in other courses which left them with a sense of passivity and anxiety over teacher expectations.

REFERENCE

1. CONNOLLY, P. 1989. Writing and the ecology of learning. *In* Writing to Learn Mathematics and Science. P. Connolly & T. Vilardi, Eds.: 1–14. Teachers College Press. New York.

An Expert System Approach to Teaching Problem Solving in Biological Instrumentation

CLAIRE A. RINEHART

Department of Biology
Western Kentucky University
Bowling Green, Kentucky 42101

INTRODUCTION

A graduate course in biological instrumentation was designed to introduce new graduate students to the theory, operation, and limitations of instruments that are used in thesis research. In this course, students are introduced to the theory and operation of each instrument by a researcher who can serve as a future resource. Students usually get hands-on experience during the associated laboratory. Interactive computer simulations like "Subcellular Fractionation and Centrifugation"[1] and "Protein Purification"[2] have been very useful in extending the experience of centrifugation and column chromatography beyond the limited laboratory exercise. Towards the end of this course, however, students need to learn to integrate their knowledge of individual instruments into a process of solving more complex research problems in which the sequential use of several instruments or methods are required. In view of this need, I have developed an interactive system similar to those above that covered most of the instruments covered in the course.

MATERIALS AND METHODS

The interactive system was developed using HyperCard[3] and runs on Apple Macintosh computers. Each screen contains windows for the *question,* the *list of instruments,* the list of *instruments selected* and the *response.* Whenever a problem is started, parameters are initialized that will direct the flow of valid options. After reading the problem in the *question* window, students select instruments in the order that they feel will solve the problem from the *list of instruments* window. After each instrument selection the current parameters are checked against the rules for that instrument. If there is a match, then the parameters are changed to reflect progress in the process and an appropriate response is returned in the *response* window to inform the user of the progress made. If a match is not found, then the parameters remain the same and the user is informed that no progress was made. Each time an instrument selection is made, the name of the instrument is added to the end of the list in the *instrument selected* window. Those selections with matching rules have an asterisk placed before the name in the *instrument selected* window. This allows the student to review the flow of previous valid and invalid choices. When students have traversed a valid course of instruments, the program informs them that they have completed the problem and moves to the next problem screen.

RESULTS AND DISCUSSION

I have used this system for three semesters with classes of eight to ten students. All but one student indicated that it was useful in helping them see how the instruments could work together in a research environment. I found that most students needed to try two or three problems before they felt comfortable with the system and the interactive approach. Review of the order and types of instruments chosen by a student (listed in the *instrument selected* window) was useful in evaluating their knowledge of each instrument's proper use as well as their skill level in problem solving.

REFERENCES

1. SMITH, K. R. & B. D. HAMES. 1988. Subcellular Fractionation and Centrifugation: A Strategic Approach. IRL Press. Oxford, England.
2. BOOTH, A. G. & B. D. HAMES. 1987. Protein Purification. IRL Press. Oxford, England.
3. HyperCard. 1991. Version 2.1. Apple Computer, Inc. Cupertino, CA.

Life in Space: An Undergraduate Seminar Experience

M. A. ROKITKA

Department of Physiology
School of Medicine and Biomedical Sciences
State University of New York
Buffalo, New York 14214

Physiological adaptation is the unifying theme for a "systems approach" seminar offered to groups of 20 students enrolled in the University Honors Program. In this seminar, students participate in discussion-oriented classroom sessions designed to consider the nature of the space environment, the challenges it offers to living organisms, and the multiple adjustments that organisms make when introduced into space. A book dealing with survival in space serves as the basic course resource[1]; it introduces students to the physical aspects of space and considers the physiological impact implied by them. The text is used extensively early in the course as the basis for small group discussions and problem solving exercises.

COURSE FEATURES

Numerous collaborative learning strategies are used throughout the course. Students generate their own hypotheses, share them with a partner, and proceed to form small groups whose task is to refine the hypotheses and design tests for them. This "think-pair-share" technique is used in preparing hypothetical proposals as responses to announcements of spaceflight research opportunities. A "pass-a-problem" technique is used as a brainstorming activity: students indicate the topic of their assigned paper or presentation on an index card, and these are passed from student to student as they make suggestions regarding content, use of audio/visual materials, and references. "Peer review" is a feature which follows small group presentations: students evaluate each other on the basis of content, effective use of audio/visual material, and communication skills. "Role playing" engages student volunteers in the reenactment of an actual interview conducted by Soviet reporters. Student reporters question student cosmonauts who spent one year in the weightlessness of space. This exercise is a unique way of presenting the long-term effects of exposure to zero gravity without delivering a traditional lecture. Finally, groups of students are challenged to use their imagination and ingenuity as they become "stranded in space." By engaging students in a "consensus exercise" which demands group decisions, this activity evokes group dynamics that ultimately result in survival and rescue from a life-threatening situation.

Students prepare both oral and written presentations on selected space topics. They are encouraged to be creative and to make liberal use of library resources. They also collaborate on small group presentations which focus on any one of five major physiological systems known to make profound adaptations to the space environment.

The occasional use of videotapes brings space into the classroom. Students observe inflight conditions and reactions, list their observations, and offer speculations. During the most recent offering of this course, a recent nine-day shuttle mission (Spacelab Life Sciences 1, June 1991) served as the primary focus of the course. During an earlier course offering, visits by an astronaut-in-training and conference calls with astronauts enabled students to solicit answers to their questions about the space experience.

The uniqueness of this seminar course offering and a general fascination with space undoubtedly account for the positive evaluations it has received. Students learn a great deal of normal human, animal, and plant physiology within the context of a course dealing with an extreme environment.

REFERENCE

1. HARDING, R. 1989. Survival in Space: Medical Problems of Manned Spaceflight. Routledge. New York.

ABASE: A Multi-Component Computer Program to Teach Acid-Base Regulation[a]

A. ROVICK, J. MICHAEL, AND J. LI

Rush Medical College
Chicago, Illinois 60612
and
Illinois Institute of Technology
Chicago, Illinois 60616

To understand acid-base (AB) regulation, students must understand the behavior of the component subsystems and their underlying mechanisms, be able to mentally integrate the functions of individual components into a unified control system, and have a way to represent the events that occur in response to an acid-base disturbance. This requires that they have a chance to practice applying their knowledge and understanding to the solution of problems. The computer program ABASE assists students to do these things—it is not, however, intended to provide initial instruction.

ABASE consists of four lessons, which interactively review these topics: buffers, respiratory and renal compensation, and the Davenport nomogram (DN). Although students are expected to have studied these subjects before working with ABASE, they often are uncertain about their knowledge and appreciate having a chance to review some of the material. Hence, ABASE permits lessons to be done at any time: (*a*) after a student initially signs on, (*b*) after one or more problems have been done, or (*c*) even from within a problem. In the lattermost case, students can branch out of a problem and return to the same point after completing as much of a lesson as they want.

The program has seven problems (FIG. 1). Each of these represents a situation that causes acute and/or chronic acid-base changes. To solve a problem, students predict the qualitative changes (increase, decrease, no change) that occur in response to changes in five AB variables by making entries into a Predictions Table[1] (FIG. 2). They must predict changes that (1) occur in direct response to the disturbance, (2) result from respiratory compensation, (3) are present at the completion of respiratory compensation, (4) are caused by renal compensation, and (5) are present in the final AB state of the subject. ABASE evaluates these predictions and gives instruction for errors that were made.

Next, the student traces the time course of the AB response on a DN by plotting points that represent the acid-base status of the subject in the procedure at each of the time periods represented in the Predictions Table. Student errors are once again critiqued and instruction is provided as necessary. Finally,

[a]This work has been supported by the Cognitive Science Program, ONR Grant N00014-91-J-1622 GAN AA1711319.

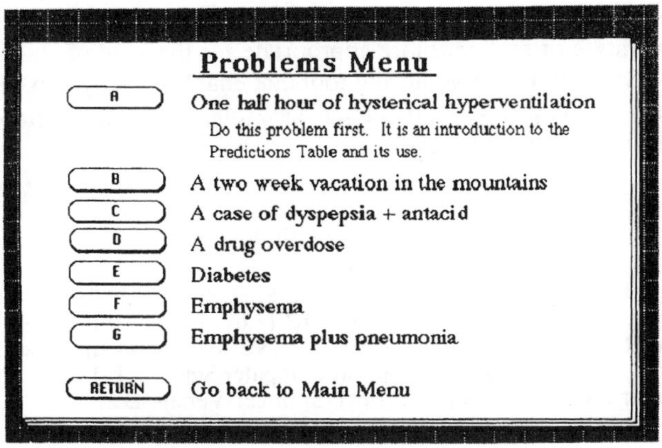

FIGURE 1. The ABASE problem list.

ABASE uses animation to trace the AB response, and it summarizes the important aspects of the physiological response as well.

ABASE has a dictionary of terms: users can branch to this dictionary as desired by clicking the mouse button. After finishing with the dictionary, the student can return to the original point in the program with another mouse click.

Teachers often like the major features of a particular teaching program while not being entirely pleased with the author's questions, explanations, or the

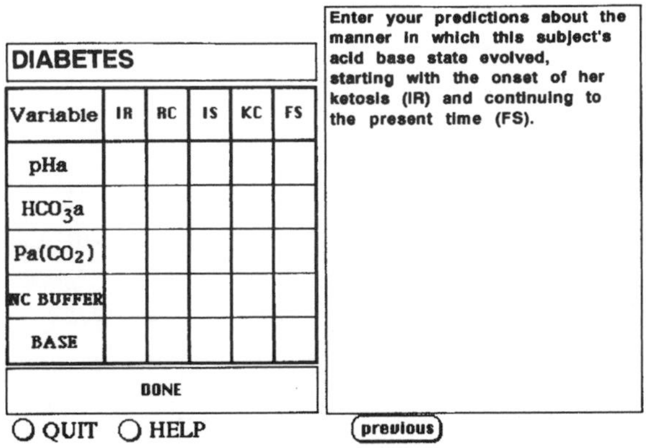

FIGURE 2. The ABASE Predictions Table. The student predicts the qualitative effects ($\uparrow$ = increase, $\downarrow$ = decrease, 0 = no change) of the procedure or condition (in this case, diabetes) on the variables listed in the first column. These predictions must be made for all of the time periods shown in columns 2–6 (IR = initial response [includes buffering], RC = respiratory compensation, IS = intermediate state [the condition following RC], KC = renal compensation, FS = final state). ABASE will use these predictions as the basis for the instruction that it provides the student.

tactics employed by the program, and they wish that they could personalize it to their own style or make it more appropriate for the kind of student that they teach. ABASE contains an authoring tool that enables teachers to easily modify existing lessons or problems or create new ones.[2] No programming skill is required to make these changes.

REFERENCES

1. ROVICK, A. A. & J. A. MICHAEL. 1992. The Predictions Table: A tool for assessing students' knowledge. Am. J. Physiol. **263** (Adv. Physiol. Ed. 8): S33–36.
2. LI, J., A. ROVICK & J. MICHAEL. 1992. ABASE: A hypermedia-based tutoring and authoring system. *In* Lecture Notes in Computer Science. I. Tomek, Ed.: 380–390. Computer Assisted Learning (series). Springer-Verlag. Berlin.

Teaching Concept Mapping

DEE U. SILVERTHORN

Department of Zoology
University of Texas
Austin, Texas 78712

Concept mapping is a non-linear way of organizing material which was first introduced into science education in the late 1970s and early 1980s.[1-3] A map consists of concepts (items or events) linked by arrows labelled to explain the relationship between the connected terms. The most general or most inclusive terms are placed at the top of the map, with each descending level containing material that is more and more specific. The advantage of a concept map over a traditional outline is its nonlinearity. A good concept map will be like a road map, with arrows going in all directions to tie together related concepts. Since lectures and textbooks present material in a linear fashion, students may lose track of the fact that material currently under discussion has some relationship to topics covered previously. Concept maps with their horizontal and branching linkages provide an opportunity for students to explore complex relationships in a biological system.

Students can be provided with teacher-prepared maps, but the real benefit of mapping comes about when students prepare their own maps. By arranging the material themselves, students question the relationships between terms, organize concepts into a hierarchical structure, and look for similarities and differences between items. Teaching students how to concept map is important since it is probably an unfamiliar process and they may not know how to begin. The instructor introduces mapping by explaining the parts and structure of a map. Students are assigned a familiar topic (living organisms, the cell, the forest) and asked to make individual maps. Several student maps are then drawn on the board and discussed to show the students that (*a*) there is no "right" way to draw a map as long as the relationships are correct, and that (*b*) maps are as individual as the people who draw them. For beginning students, the instructor may provide a list of concepts to be mapped. More advanced students can design their own maps. Once the maps are discussed, the instructor assigns the students to small groups in which they compare, critique, and revise their maps. Some groups may elect to make a composite group map. Two key points to the instruction are: (1) students make individual maps first, and (2) students compare maps in small groups. The small group work points out incorrect linkages between terms and reminds students of concepts and links they may have forgotten to include on their individual maps. Examples of good and bad student maps are shown in FIGURES 1 and 2.

Once students are comfortable with this type of concept map, they may move into more complex mapping strategies. The students select a major unit of information such as photosynthesis or the cardiovascular system. They then integrate everything they learned in the unit into a single giant map on a piece of poster board. These complex maps may include anatomical drawings and

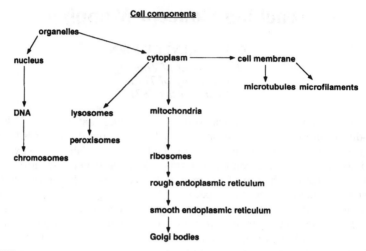

FIGURE 1. A student concept map of "the cell" with no hierarchy and poor linkages. Linking arrows are not labelled and the relationships between linked concepts are unclear or incorrect.

figures in addition to concepts with linking arrows. The giant system maps force students to literally construct the "big picture." When done correctly, students use the all-inclusive maps in place of other study notes. For instructors, the maps provide quick insight into the way a student is thinking about a subject.

Students who use mapping consistently are enthusiastic about the usefulness of mapping in both science and liberal arts classes. They feel that they understand the material better and retain the information longer because they had to

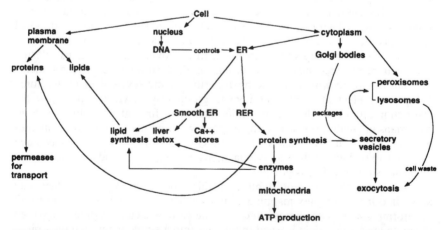

FIGURE 2. An excellent student map which demonstrates complex understanding of the relationship between the structures and functions of a cell. Linking arrows are labelled if their meaning might be unclear. Horizontal links tie related concepts together.

analyze the concepts and their relationships in order to construct a map that made sense.

REFERENCES

1. STEWART, J., J. VAN KIRK & R. ROWELL. 1979. Concept maps: A tool for use in biology teaching. Am. Biol. Teacher **41(3):** 171–175.
2. ARNAUDIN, M. W., J. J. MINTZES, C. S. DUNN & T. H. SHAFER. 1984. Concept mapping in college science teaching. J. Coll. Sci. Teaching **14(2):** 117–121.
3. NOVAK, J. D. & D. B. GOWIN. 1984. Learning How to Learn. Cambridge University Press. New York.

Macintosh Computers and MacLab Data Acquisition Units in Animal Physiology Teaching Laboratories

PHILIP J. STEPHENS

Department of Biology
Villanova University
Villanova, Pennsylvania 19085

Studies have shown that computer-assisted instruction (CAI) helps students learn quicker,[1,3] especially when it is used to augment traditional instruction.[2,4] Since the undergraduate Animal Physiology course at Villanova University uses traditional lectures to present new material and laboratory sessions to subsequently illustrate major principles, CAI has been integrated into the teaching laboratories.

A Macintosh SE computer is used at each work station, and the six computers use LocalTalk to communicate with the server in the departmental network. Interactive HyperCard software programs have been developed to replace the laboratory handouts, so that the computers are used as a source of information and instruction. The HyperCard application is opened when the

Topic		Report	Survey	Topic		Report	Survey
1 Tour IntroLab Word Processing		H	H	**6** Mouse Thyroid		√	H
2 Size and metabolism		√	H	**7** Human ECG		√	H
3 Membrane Potentials		√	H	**8** Frog Heart		√	H
4 Think Tank Chart Intro		H	H	**9** Human Lung		√	H
5 Frog Striated muscle		√	H	**10** Human Kidney		√	H

Animal Physiology Home Card — Quit

FIGURE 1. The "Home Card." This card is divided into ten numbered boxes; each corresponds to a laboratory exercise and is covered by a transparent button. The mouse is moved to position the cursor in a particular box and then clicked once to open that program. The word-processing program for each laboratory exercise is opened by clicking on the "Report" button. The Hypercard program is terminated by clicking on the "Quit" button.

142

computer is turned on and the "Home Card" is displayed on the screen (FIG. 1). The student moves the mouse and clicks on the appropriate topic to open the program or "LabStack" (FIG. 2). Students navigate through the LabStack by using the mouse to move the cursor and to click on buttons and fields. Key words in the text are set in bold typeface and are overlaid by buttons, which are linked to cards containing additional information presented as text, diagrams, and animated sequences. This additional information outlines theory, the use of equipment, expected results, and details on how to perform tasks such as data analysis. The flexibility inherent within the programs and the system of "information layering" allows students to customize their learning experience, since they control the speed and depth of study.

A MacLab/4 data acquisition unit has been added to each work station. The MacLab/4 unit and its associated software permit the analog output from standard laboratory instruments to be displayed on the computer screen in chart recorder or oscilloscope format. The student clicks on a button to open the recording application from within the HyperCard program, and the 4 megabytes of RAM allows the computer to run the HyperCard and the recording applications concurrently; the student uses the Applications icon to select the application to be displayed on the screen. Data analysis is software-driven and does not

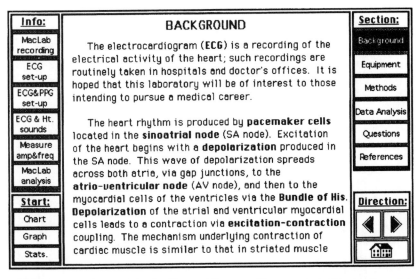

FIGURE 2. The first card in the Human Electrocardiogram stack. The stack contains cards with the same basic layout. The text is found in the middle and contains certain words in bold type; this indicates a button which is linked to one or more cards with information on that topic. Buttons in the right margin allow the user to move around the stack, either sequentially (by using the arrow keys), or directly to one of the six sections; clicking on the Home icon returns the user to the Home stack. "Info" Buttons in the upper left margin are linked to cards that provide information that may be needed at any time during the laboratory exercise, while those in the bottom left margin open the MacLab recording software ("Chart"), the graphics, and the statistics applications.

require the MacLab unit, so students can perform sophisticated analysis of their data file on any Macintosh computer with the appropriate software.

REFERENCES

1. BELFRY, M. J. & P. H. WINNE. 1988. A review of the effectiveness of computer-based instruction in nursing education. Computers in Nursing **6:** 77–85.
2. GUNDY, G. C. 1990. Hypercard-based teaching: Preliminary experiences and research in anatomy and physiology courses. Collegiate Microcomputer **8:** 287–292.
3. KULIK, C.-L. C. & J. A. KULIK. 1991. Effectiveness of computer-based instruction: An updated analysis. Computers in Human Behavior **7:** 75–94.
4. MOORE, L., D. WECHTER & L. ARONOW. 1991. Assessing the effectiveness of computer-assisted instruction in a pharmacology course. Acad. Med. **66:** 194–196.

Problem Solving, Expertise, and Artificial Neural Networks

RON STEVENS AND ALINA LOPO

Department of Microbiology and Immunology
UCLA School of Medicine
Los Angeles, California 90024

There is a strong need for computer-based simulations and interpretive evaluation tools that can be applied to multiple disciplines where expertise is beginning to be developed and that can begin to model how a student acquires, stores and processes knowledge. Our previous studies of the problem solving processes of medical students have shown that successful and non-successful problem solutions can be readily distinguished by search path mapping where the progression of individual students, or groups of students, through the problem solving process is recorded and graphically displayed.[1] Successful approaches are characterized by patterns of focused test selections centered in the relevant content area whereas unsuccessful solutions often display patterns more consistent with searching and failure to recognize or interpret relevant data.

While providing insight into how students approach and search for solutions to problems, these studies had limitations. For instance, the search path map patterns were generated *after* a student had completed a problem: this makes it difficult to detect misconceptions during the problem solving process and to provide real-time remediation. Additionally, for maximum usefulness, the search path map patterns must be viewed and interpreted by an expert. What is more important, while search path maps reveal patterns of successful and non-successful solutions, the quantification of this information was difficult. However, the presence of distinctive patterns of successful problem solutions suggested that perhaps a variant of search path mapping could be implemented—one that utilized artificial neural network software. Supervised neural networks build models which classify patterns or make decisions according to patterns of inputs and outputs they have "learned" from training on multiple sample patterns. In the studies to be presented, we have trained artificial neural networks to recognize the successful performances of students on multiple immunology and infectious disease simulations. These neural networks classified subsequent students' performances as successful or non-successful more than ninety percent of the time. When the output weights for successful performances were examined following each test solution, there was a progressive increase in the outputs for the relevant problem and low values for the remaining problems (FIG. 1). These results suggested that at a minimum, artificial neural network analysis of students' problem solving performances could identify problem solving success and failure.

The trained neural networks could also provide information as to why the problem solving process failed. Problem solving can be divided into multiple components, including the generation of hypotheses, the gathering of information, the integration of information, and the evaluation of hypotheses in light of

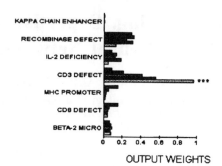

OUTPUT WEIGHTS

FIGURE 1. Case-Specific Output Weights Following Sequential Test Selections of Successful Problem Solutions. Each student's test selection was given an input weight of 1 and entered as test data into the trained neural network for classification. The resulting neural network output weights for each of the cases were then obtained and the process was repeated for each test selection until the completion of the problem. For each case category the top bar is the output weight following the first test selection and the lowest bar is the output weight following the last test selection. Student test selections not included in the classifying characteristics are indicated by blank values.

*** indicates the case being solved.

the new information. The inability to formulate a hypothesis would be reflected in the failure to choose relevant data in a directed manner. This would be revealed by extensive searching for information and failure to recognize relevant data when chosen. We have previously observed this form of problem solving difficulty using search path mapping.[1] When such students' performances are processed by the neural network on a test-by-test basis, the output weights (as expected) show little selectivity for either the case being solved or any of the additional cases (FIG. 2A).

In evaluating multiple students' unsuccessful performances we often (40% of failed attempts) observed that the neural network output weights indicated a "good" solution to a problem, *but it was the wrong problem* (FIG. 2B). These results suggest that a directed, yet inappropriate, approach to the case solution may often contribute to a student's missing a problem.

The above data raise the possibility that a process of bias, analogy, or pattern matching may occur in cases where the students attempts to map the solution of a current problem to another, previously performed problem.[2]

The above approach is applicable to a broad number of situations where expertise is beginning to be developed and may be useful for determining how students acquire, store, and process knowledge.

REFERENCES

1. STEVENS, R. H., J. M. McCOY & A. R. KWAK. Solving the problem of how medical students solve problems. M.D. Computing 1991:13.
2. STEVENS, R. H. & K. NAJAFI. 1992. Students' use of prior problem representations when performing computer-based simulations: An artificial neural network perspective. Acad. Med. **67:** S51.

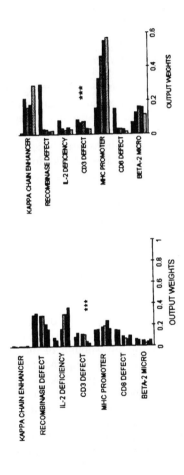

FIGURE 2. Case-specific output weights following sequential test selections of nonsuccessful problem solutions. Each student's test selection was given an input weight of 1 and entered as test data into the trained neural network for classification. The resulting neural network output weights for each of the cases were then obtained and the process was repeated for each test selection until the completion of the problem. For each case category the top bar is the output weight following the first test selection and the lowest bar is the output weight following the last test selection. Student test selections not included in the classifying characteristics are indicated by blank values. *** indicates the case being solved.

Promoting Active Learning
in the Lecture Hall

P. J. WILKIN[a] AND J. W. VANABLE, JR.[b]

aBiology/Chemistry Section
Purdue University North Central
Westville, Indiana 46391-9528
bDepartment of Biological Sciences
Lilly Hall
Purdue University
West Lafayette, Indiana 47907

Holding students' attention and accurately transmitting information are enhanced by (*a*) providing each student in advance with materials representing an incomplete outline of the lecture, and (*b*) including (as appropriate concepts) key experiments and data, as well as diagrams of structures. Then, in the lecture, one "clothes the skeleton": on overhead-transparency copies of the sheets given to the students, the lecturer writes and draws the additional information needed for completion. The incomplete information serves as guideposts to the students, helping them to follow the lecture and reducing their need for copying sometimes intricate diagrams. Because of the incompleteness of the furnished material, the attention of the students is needed for producing notes that are useful. The lecture becomes a detective story in which the student follows the trail of clues. Describing key experiments emphasizes the experimental basis of biology. Demonstrations also involve students in the lecture. The application of these principles is illustrated by an example: the sodium channel of nerve and muscle.[1]

FIGURE 1 is given to the students. The amount of the following information that is written on the overhead transparency would depend upon the objectives of the course (sometimes even more information would be added as needed). FIGURE 1 depicts the main, alpha, protein subunit of the channel; its gene is cloned, the clone is isolated, analyzed for base sequence (and thus protein amino acid sequence), and a model is made of the probable folding and placement of the protein in the cell membrane. In the upper left part, mRNAs from the electric organ of the electric eel are used to produce, by recombination, complementary DNA (cDNA) bacterial clones. The clones containing the sodium-channel cDNA are isolated by the use of DNA probes, based upon partial amino acid sequencing of the sodium-channel protein, itself isolated from the electric organ by the use of labelled channel-specific binding toxin (upper right part of figure). Base sequencing of the cDNA leads to the amino acid sequence of the channel alpha protein, revealing 1,820 amino acid residues in four homologous domains, numbered I to IV. (Only domain IV is shown in the mid part of FIGURE 1.) A hydropathy plot of the amino acid sequence of the protein, and the number of amino acids in each peak of the plot, suggests that each domain crosses the membrane six times as an α-helix (S1 to S5). Genetic manipulation of the channel protein has implicated the regions between helixes S5 and S6 as lining

148

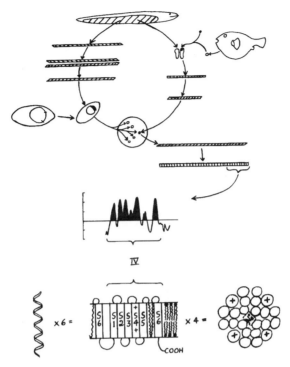

FIGURE 1. The determination of the structure of the sodium channel by sequencing cDNA.

the aqueous pore, and making the selectivity filter. The fourth subunit in each domain (S4) is positively charged (every third residue is a basic lysine or arginine) and may be the voltage-sensing part of the molecule. During channel activation the outward movement of S4, by a screw-type rotation, could cause the gating current. The channel protein must sit stably in the membrane phospholipid bilayer, so that the outer parts of the channel have nonpolar regions facing outward.

Many demonstrations are possible during the course of the lecture by way of reinforcing the information transmitted to the students. An electric eel would be a remarkable contribution, but photos of the eel and puffer fish would be useful. Any part of the experimental procedures could be demonstrated. Any of the molecules described in the figure, but particularly the channel protein, could be modeled.

REFERENCE

1. HILLE, B. 1992. Ionic Channels of Excitable Membranes (2nd ed.). Sinauer Associates. Sunderland, MA.

Index of Contributors

151